Masonic Tombstones and Masonic Secrets

**To John Cooper,
friend and freemason**

Masonic Tombstones and Masonic Secrets

Dora C. Jett's
Minor Sketches of Major Folk

Edited and introduced by
Paul Rich

WESTPHALIA PRESS
An imprint of Policy Studies Organization

Masonic Tombstones and Masonic Secrets
Dora C. Jett's
Minor Sketches of Major Folk

Copyright © 2012 by Policy Studies Organization

Westphalia Press
An imprint of Policy Studies Organization
dgutierrezs@ipsonet.org

All rights reserved. No part of this book may be
reproduced or transmitted in any form or by any means
graphic, electronic, or mechanical, including
photocopying, recording, taping, or by any information
storage or retrieval system, without the permission in
writing from the publisher.

For information:
Westphalia Press
1527 New Hampshire Ave., N.W.
Washington, D.C. 20036

ISBN-13: 978-0944285718
ISBN-10: 0944285716

Updated material and comments on this edition can be
found at the Policy Studies Organization website:
http://www.ipsonet.org/

Preface to the New Edition

Masonic Tombstones and Masonic Secrets:
Dora C. Jett's *Minor Sketches of Major Folk*

The axiom that we take our secrets to the grave is not entirely true, as our graves may reveal some secrets. Such is the case with Masonic graveyards. Secrecy and ritual are two characteristics of some American voluntary associations that deserve study.[i] Research into the subject enables scholars and students to better understand volunteerism. Considering how widespread such groups are, involving all kinds of people and in many countries, it is surprising how little is known about them. Social scientists who give more attention to this aspect of popular culture will be rewarded by the results, and one way to proceed is through cemeteries.

When we walk around an old graveyard, there are many odd symbols on the stones, and they often relate to fraternal groups: "…the Shriners, the Order of the Eastern Star, the International Order of Job's Daughters, the Order of the Golden Chain, the Order of the Amaranth, the Prince Hall organisation, not to mention the Mystic Order of Veiled Prophets of the Enchanted Realm!!, The Ancient Egyptian Order of Sciots!! Or the Order of the White Shrine of Jerusalem. And I assure you that this little list has hardly scratched the surface!"[ii]

The differences between countries and regions can be large. For example, the Odd Fellows, which in the United States and England have always been a lower middle class movement, are elitist in Scandinavia. The Orange Order, such a disturbing political influence in modern day Ireland, was primarily social in the United States.

The Masons are the oldest of these societies and the Masonic Cemetery recorded in this book is part of the legacy of Fredericksburg Lodge #4 A.F. & A.M. The site was donated to the lodge in 1784 by James Somerville, a Scottish merchant and mayor of Fredericksburg. It possesses the bible on which George Washington took his Masonic Obligations, a punch bowl used by the Marquis de Lafayette, and a Gilbert Stuart painting of Washington.

He or she will also encounter vast amounts of allegory and metaphor, so that without an advance immersion in the rituals the text will be unintelligible. The symbolism employed requires the researcher to be thoroughly prepared before confronting archives or tombstones. Still another difficulty in the case of these enigmatic groups is that both members and non-members have been guilty of fabrications and falsifications to advance their claims of antiquity and importance.

Nevertheless, fraternal graveyards, and Masonic ones in particular, suggest a vast amount of untapped archival material for research. Depending on the packrat mentality of individual lodge secretaries, there can be treasure troves of menus, sheet music, visiting cards, membership applications, correspondence with sister affiliates in other countries, and of course, minutes by the ton. Since many chapters and lodges had an ethnic or vocational aspect, the possibilities for projects with an international and economic aspect are more numerous than would first appear to be the case.[iii]

While Masonry is a prominent example of the potential for scholarship that this field of inquiry offers, other organizations provide equally interesting research possibilities. Every cemetery has its own unique mix: the Sons of Norway do not have the same geographical distribution as the Knights of Pythias. Studies of international relationships within and between such movements are waiting to be done, as well as research into the way in which they served specific nationality and religious groups. They were not always exclusive, but inclusive, and also have served as facilitators of multiculturalism, helping integrate the community around a pluralistic ideal, while admittedly at other times they have been extremely divisive. Ms. Jett captures with entertaining vignettes the life of one such community.

Paul Rich, *George Mason University*

ⁱ Members of what appear to be secret societies, including those in Masonic organizations, often assert that matters are not secret but 'discrete'. Allen E. Roberts, *Freemasonry in American History*, Macoy Publishing, Richmond (Virginia), 1985, 1. "Secrecy", *Royal Arch Mason*, Vol.18 No.4, Winter 1994, 118.

ⁱⁱ ' Henry Engelsman, "From the Editor's Chair", *The Diadem*, April 1994, No.14, 1.

ⁱⁱⁱ Unfortunately, the Masons themselves have not produced as much research as one could expect. "The level of research within the Craft is low, and mostly concerns the local history of lodges or remembrance of folk heroes or other famous Americans who were freemasons." Michel Brodsky, "Breaking the Ring", privately circulated advance copy of lecture to Quatuor Coronati Lodge No. 2076, 10 November 1994, 3.

THE
MADONNA
OF THE
RAPPAHANNOCK
from the PAINTING by
GARI MELCHERS
COURTESY of
Hon. JOHN BARTON PAYNE

The home of this eminent artist is Belmont, on the Rappahannock River. It was also the home in an early day of Susannah Stuart Fitzhugh Knox. Where Mr. Melchers' studio now stands was once the playground of little William A. Knox and his big sister, Anna Campbell Knox, afterwards the wife of Bazil Gordon.

MINOR SKETCHES

OF

MAJOR FOLK

and where they sleep

The Old Masonic Burying Ground

Fredericksburg, Virginia

By DORA C. JETT

Author of "In Tidewater Virginia"

JUDITH FRANCES CHINN

and

CHARLES LEROY CONWAY

with affectionate remembrance

Foreword

These are the days when commendable effort is being made to throw the searchlight on every phase of the past. There seems an omnipresent desire to lift the shadowy curtain of time, light the dark places behind, and glimpse the bearing and customs of those oft-times worthy men and women, to whom this generation owes much. There is truth in the old proverb, "The glory of the children are their fathers."

With what keen pleasure would the whole universe respond to that genius who could by some inventive process put upon the screen, if only for a short duration of time, the true home life, and the social and the military life of such worthies as rest in the old Masonic Cemetery! No important epoch in the nation's life and no individual characteristic need be omitted. Every epoch and every characteristic is represented.

Conspicuous in the train is the major in the Revolution, Benjamin Day, and the "mere boy" of the same period, John Minor, afterwards General Minor, in the War of 1812. Others of like interest pass in review, and then General Lewis Littlepage appears, and presently Susan Savage—the environment of both reveals, though in widely divergent callings, the significance of an American's labors in foreign fields.

And who are these infants so closely associated with that surgeon in the Confederate States navy? They are, each and all, the grandchildren of Princeton's hero, General Hugh Mercer. Other pleasing pictures pass, and scenes from old Dumfries arrest one's attention, for here is Mrs. Delia Forbes Smith, the grandmother of one Mrs. William K. Vanderbilt, with a portrayal of beguiling Scotch customs, brought with her ancestors from across the wide waters.

Reverend John Woodville, in clerical robes of the eighteenth century, and Colonel John Stanard, with his corps of men in attendance upon the great Lafayette at Spotsylvania Courthouse, in 1824, are pictures upon which one loves to linger. The children, grandchildren, and great-grandchildren of that worthy couple, William and Susannah Fitzhugh Knox—the progenitors of many Gordons, Fitzhughs, Knoxes, and others, who have added distinction to many of the arts and professions practiced in this section and elsewhere—pass and repass amongst the others; some with the dignity of years and importance, and others in pinafores and sunbonnets. And who is this whose air is so

suggestive of the true Virginia gentleman?
It is Mayor Robert Lewis, the nephew, and
at one time, the private secretary of General
Washington, and the son of Fielding and
Betty Lewis.

Interesting and picturesque Scotch customs and characteristics are revealed in the
domestic and business activities of thrifty
Bazil Gordon, the "Blair Brothers, Import-
ers," and the wealthy old bachelor, James
Somerville. The great niece of Sir Alexander Spotswood recalls to one's mind that
romantic expedition across the mountains
with the jolly Knights of the Golden Horse-
shoe.

All these are here and many more.

I shall not attempt to thank the many in-
dividuals for their generous help in the com-
pilation of these vague outlines, nor to name
the various libraries, books and records from
which was culled my information. But without those time-worn documents at Fredericksburg, Spotsylvania, and Stafford court-
houses this small volume would have been
impossible.

It is hoped that the reader of these little
sketches will enjoy them in the same pro-
portion as did the writer in collecting them.

Dora C. Jett.

April, 1928.

Major Names of Minor Mention

—

Illustrations

MINOR SKETCHES

OF

MAJOR FOLK

They were of fame, and had been glorious in another day.—BYRON.

Entrance to Masonic Cemetery. James Monroe's Law Office on the right.

Minor Sketches
of
Major Folk

"Here may thy storm-bett vessel safely ride,
This is the port of rest from troublous toyle,
The world's sweet inn from paine and wearisome
    turmoyle . . . ."
Spencer's Fairy Queen.

That this is a happier, more carefree, less sentimental, more optimistic, and more practical age than some periods of the ages gone before, is suggested by many of the sober epitaphs on the stones of the worthies who sleep in the old burying-ground of Fredericksburg Lodge, No. 4, A. F. and A. M. Mourning mothers rejoice because their precious babies have passed from pain to happiness, and heart-broken wives who gloried in their husband's achievements have only one incentive to live—the hope of a short-lived separation. But absolute confidence in the expectation of a happy reunion is the carrying note, and supplies the comforting word of optimism.

The old stone wall—a type of early days—is divided on Charles Street to allow iron gates to form the entrance. Inside of the enclosure, to the left, a splendid black walnut tree lifts its leafy limbs to heaven, and a young mimosa is not far away, while at intervals, linden, locust, elm and maple trees, planted in recent years, dot the surface of this blessed little spot, and an occasional bed of blossoms breaks the continuity of the level green sward.

This grassy little plot measures its size by about one-third of a city block, and is now, and has been for several years, tenderly cared for by the Masonic Lodge. It is one of the many ancient and interesting possessions of that time-honored body—the lodge in which George Washington was initiated, passed a Fellow Craft, and raised a Master Mason, and in which he held his membership for life. The ground was acquired from an early member, about the time of the Revolution. James Somerville, one of those splendid types of man who dignify the pages of our early history,—for him and others like him we still extend our thanks to Scotland,—made his will, "being wrote with my own hand this 23rd day of February, 1798 . . ." One clause, although somewhat involved, is sufficiently clear to enable one to arrive at a correct interpretation: "Twelve or fifteen years ago, I sold to the Lodge of Freemasons of Fredericksburg, a lot or half acre of ground in said Towne known in the plan thereof by no. . . . purchased with an intention to build their Lodge thereon, hitherto has been used as a place of interment, the consideration I long ago received, a sufficient conveyance is I believe not made, I am and ever have been ready and willing to secure this property. In case this is not done before I depart this life, I request and enjoin my Executors, may have a good and safe title made to my Brethren of the Lodge, in such manner as may be found most effectually and expedient . . . The lot I purchased of Wilkerson and wife . . ."

Memorial stones often bear a meaningful message—a dependable, accurate, and significant message. Many of these representing notable persons in Fredericksburg annals. are scattered through the various burial plots in and around the town. It is a matter of regret that they are so scattered. Perhaps the names in this little tract, which tradition insists was part of the grounds surrounding the residence of James Somerville, justify more than any other particular spot, the pride which the residents feel in its past citizenry. The quaint brick building on Charles

Street, directly across from the Masonic
Cemetery, now used as an electrical shop, is
said to be a part of the ancient home of
James Somerville. The mammoth fireplace,
with stout cranes on either side, still to be
seen in one of the rooms, carries one back to
a distant day, when perhaps this old kitchen
added a necessary and enjoyable service to
the welfare of James Somerville and his
good Scotch relatives and friends.

A few years ago a movement was on foot
to do away with this old graveyard and to
erect thereon a modern Masonic Lodge. The
opposition to this movement by the thinking
public,—those who have regard for those
vital concerns expressed in various ways in
this interesting acre, was, needless to say,
violent in the extreme.

Among those who opposed the plan, and
who lent his ability and his influence to the
general opposition, was the late Judge A.
W. Wallace, a gentleman of the old school
in every sense, a resident of Fredericksburg
all his long life. He told a story, which,
though it loses much in its reproduction, is
nevertheless of sufficient interest to narrate
here. At the time in which the power of his
mind was concentrated on the effacement of
what he considered a sacrilege, he was one
evening taking his customary stroll about

town, and sauntered into the old burying-ground, diagonally opposite his home. No sooner had he entered than he heard many voices of weird revelry, and all kinds of boisterous festivity, with the refrain a note of protestation which it was impossible to at once interpret. Cautiously stepping near the big tomb of General John Minor, he heard above the rollicking din the words, "No, we will never, never, never consent to being removed." From there he visited the graves of his relatives, the Gordons, and the same chorus reached his ear. Going to the flat sepulchre of Lewis Littlepage, the sound was that of a hundred voices, "This is *our* right, *our* possession, for many years, and we will not, will not be disturbed." Thinking that retreat, considering conditions, was more valorous than to remain, he resolved to get out, but in going he passed the monument of Daniel Grinnan, and even the haste with which he was retreating did not prevent the song of Daniel Grinnan and his retinue from reaching his ear: "This is the spot given us by our Brethren of the Lodge, and with God's help we will remain." At this juncture the Judge awakened, and on his arrival at his bank next morning, an attendant said, "Well, Judge, you needn't bother over your people of the old burying-ground any longer, events have shaped themselves so that the ground will not be disturbed for the erection of the Masonic Lodge."

A piece of fiction current today, printed in many American papers, and appearing in a London daily within the year, is that one of Shakespeare's pallbearers is buried in the old Masonic Cemetery in Fredericksburg. Iconoclasm, while maybe not so dangerous an element as a disregard for authenticity, is a trait not to be encouraged. But if no proof, no visible or tangible prop to support a cherished belief can be presented, that theory must be shattered because of its own weak and partly constructed basis. How the residents of the old town would like to stretch apocryphal tradition into a fact, and bury the pallbearer of that wonderful genius under the shade of the big black walnut tree! As the stout old red sandstone slab in the extreme southeastern corner of the cemetery, with no mark of an inscription legible, is the one pointed out today by the uninformed as the spot where lies the pallbearer of Shakespeare, it will not be out of place here to quote from Moncure D. Conway's article, *Hunting a Mythical Pallbearer*, in Harper's Magazine for January, 1886. He had been much interested prior to that date in reading the surprising item in various

news channels of the discovery of the tombstone of one of Shakespeare's pallbearers,
and this in an old burying-ground in the vicinity of his old home—Fredericksburg.

He determined as soon as time permitted
to run down this interesting myth—which he
felt sure the story would prove. He tells in
his graphic and entertaining way of his
search. Various logical deductions proved to
him the improbability of this being the burial
place of such a man. But every myth has a
basis, and the basis was the goal of his investigations. He compares the hunt for a
myth ("glorious sport!") to the fox who successfully doubled on the red-coated sports-
men at a "Cotswold meet," and says, "A
myth is as much a living organism as a fox,
as fleet and more cunning. It hides in the
bush of popular superstition, takes the color
of local pride, and enlists the truthful in its
stratagems . . ." After an exhaustive search
for the Helder stone,—the name of the mythical pallbearer was Edmond Helder,—in
various burying-grounds, he goes to the
Masonic graveyard, where a newspaper correspondent has found, "a red sandstone slab,
'Here lies interred the body of Edmond Helder . . . Obiit March 11, 1618. One of the
pallbearers of Shakespeare, the Bard of
the Avon.' This stone now lies under a

locust, the old English lettering dim but traceable." Mr. Conway says, "There is but one red sandstone slab in that graveyard; it never lay on its back . . . and there has not been for many years the faintest inscription upon it, the whole facing having come off in flakes. This perhaps the only stone in the ground about which nothing is known, was naturally fixed upon by our foxy myth as a good bush to hide in . . ." It is not surprising that Mr. Conway after such careful and laborious investigation discovered the foundation upon which the story was built. He found that out on Potomac Run in Stafford county an old stone had been unearthed during the War Between the States, with the following inscription: "Here lies the body of Edmond Helder, prectitioner in Physick and Chyrurgery. Born in Bedfordshire, Obiit March 11, 1618, Atatis sua 76." Mr. Conway suggests that some correspondent might have added that Dr. Helder was a contemporary of Shakespeare and might have attended his funeral. A printer may have incorporated the comment in the epitaph, and thus the simple comment evolved into the startling statement. It has been the means of discovering the oldest English epitaph on the American continent, according to Mr. Conway. A part of this old stone has been housed for years in the Mary Washington house.

It is a known fact that many of those conspicuous in the making of Fredericksburg's worthy history, and in some cases the nation's history, sleep in this hallowed precinct with never a word to tell their name or of their fame. It matters little to them. They have attained their material goal,

"A rest for weary pilgrims found,
They softly lie and sweetly sleep, low in the ground."

But posterity regrets the absence of that reliable source of information—the message on the memorial stone. The ravages of time, the wear of the elements, and in some cases, wanton carelessness, have been responsible for the disappearance of many of the stones known to have been here. But the name, at least, is perfectly legible today on those that remain. Masonic emblems are conspicuous on many. The Holy Bible, and square and compass are here, and over there the irradiated all-seeing eye, and the mystic G is seen many times.

The following names are recorded here:

ADAMS: In memory of Mary Adms [Adams] who
died March 10th, 1818.

Probably Mary Adams was a member of
the family of Jonas P. Adams, a member of
Fredericksburg Lodge.

ALEXANDER: Julia Anton, wife of Robert B. Alex-
ander and daughter of A. and C. Kale. Born
July 27th, 1833. Died July 7th, 1887.
Beloved by all who knew her.

ALEXANDER: Lutie B., only daughter of R. B. and
J. A. Alexander. Died November 7th, 1861
in her fourth year.

Dearest Lutie thou art gone.
Death has broken life's silver chain;
But to heaven thy spirit's flown,
Where we hope to meet again.

ALEXANDER: In memory of Margaret Timberlake
Alexander. Died July 3rd, 1900, in her 79th
year. True to her God and the Southland.

Many of the older residents of Fredericksburg remember with affection their old friend
and relative, "Aunt Peg Alexander." Her
home was in the row of brick dwellings on

Main Street, near Charlotte. She was before her marriage to Capt. Alexander, Margaret Benson Timberlake. The phrase on her tombstone is indeed indicative of her character. She was also loyal in her duty to her relatives, and very clannish, but not selfishly so, and never was there a truer friend, especially to those who needed the services of a friend.

One of her ways of expressing her fidelity to the Southland was to name two handsome trees on her pavement to Southern leaders. The act of uprooting trees on Main Street had just become a popular fad, and "Aunt Peg" firmly declared that if "Lee" and "Jackson" were taken down, it would be done over her lifeless body. They remained stoutly standing until after her death, when they were hewn down by the ruthless and unsentimental hand of "progress."

ALEXANDER: Captain R. H. Alexander, Co. C, 30th Virginia Regiment. Born Oct. 9th, 1809. Died July 28th, 1891.

This is the husband of Margaret Alexander. After the War Between the States Captain Alexander kept store on Main Street, Timberlake & Alexander being the firm name. The business of auctioneering was added to the other activities. Every characteristic of Captain Alexander was of sterling quality. He was modest and retiring in his manner, but possessed much magne-tism. It is said that his features strongly resembled those of his great chieftain, General Robert E. Lee.

ALEXANDER: In memory of Robert Brooke, 4th son of Philip T. and Lucy B. Alexander. Died Aug. 3rd, 1878 in the 66th year of his age.

Robert B. Alexander with S. Greenhow Daniel and James B. Sener were in 1850 owners and publishers of *The Democratic Recorder*, the predecessor of *The Fredericksburg Ledger*. In 1860 R. B. Alexander and Lewis O. Magrath conveyed the *Democratic Recorder* newspaper, with all its appliances, appurtenances, types, presses," etc., to George Henry Clay Rowe. The old deeds relate the story of the changes in the short life of this little sheet. Its publication was suspended during the War Between the States.

Robert Brooke Alexander was the husband of Julia Anton Kale Alexander.

ALLEN: Here lies the remains of Frances Allen, late wife of Captain James Allen, who was born the 19th Decb. 1763 and departed this life April 6th, 1799 in the 37th year of her age.

The following is taken from the *Virginia Herald* of April 9, 1799: "Died—On Saturday morning, Mrs. Allan, the amiable and worthy consort of Capt. James Allan." One feels reasonably assured that Frances Allen was amiable, though that attribute seemed the post mortem characteristic of each "relict" or "consort."

ANDERSON: Eliza Rosamond Anderson Daughter of Mary Jane and William Anderson. Born 18th Day of June 1851. Died 27th Day of June 1851.

This tiny baby was the grandchild of Captain Mathew Anderson, the child of his son William, who married Miss Faudray, of Richmond.

ANDERSON: In memory of Captain Mathew D. Anderson who departed this life Feb. 1st, 1854. A kind, affectionate husband and parent, a good neighbor, and an upright and honest man.

> The voyage of life with me is o'er
> All my sufferings have an end.
> I am at rest on that blest shore,
> With Jesus Christ, my friend.

Captain Anderson was born in Mathews county in 1794, and was of Scotch descent. His father died shortly before his birth, and his mother did not survive his infancy. He and an older brother were brought up by an uncle, whose residence was in Mathews county. Before he became of age he grew dissatisfied with an uneventful existence and inharmonious surroundings. A life on the rolling sea seemed good to him, and while a young boy, though confronted with much opposition, he became absorbed in the pursuits of the sea. The story is told and certified by a grandson of Captain Anderson, that on one occasion he deliberately upset a rowboat in the deep waters of Chesapeake Bay, in order to produce the impression that he had been drowned, and being a marvelous swimmer, he successfully made the distance to a remote sailing vessel. Incidentally the ruse produced the desired result.

His adventures in the War of 1812, in which war he became a captain, his capture of a British "prize," and the recapture of the prize, and he himself taken a prisoner to England, where he remained until 1814, is all a story of daring action. In his later years he became captain of a sailing vessel which plied the waters of the Rappahannock River, Chesapeake Bay and the Atlantic ocean as far as the West Indies. He left a large family of children and other descendents. One of his sons was Captain John K. Anderson, of the Thirtieth Virginia Regiment, Confederate army, who married Miss Ella Hundley. A son of this marriage, Fletzell Anderson, M. D., has attained distinction in his profession, practicing in this country and in London, England; and his investigations in chemistry and bacteria have made him famous in the world of science. Mary Ann Anderson, a daughter, married Robert N. Blake, of Stafford county, and their granddaughter, Maude Blake, Mrs. W. C. N. Merchant, of Chatham, Va., is the President-General, United Daughters of the Confederacy. The late W. N. Blake was a grandson. Another son, "Mat" Anderson, was proprietor of a book store here after the War Between the States.

Captain Anderson married Rosamond Reagan, who died July 19, 1855, and is sleeping near-by, but no stone marks her memory. She was fifty-seven years old.

———

BENSON: Our Mother, Mrs. Jane Benson. Born
    June 16th, 1776. Departed this life December
    1st, 1857.

Mrs. Benson was the widow of John Benson. Miss Anne Carter wrote of her as a descendant of Lady Spotswood (Mrs. John Thompson), and as, "that sweet Baptist Christian." She says Mrs. Benson's mother was a friend of Mrs. Mary Ball Washington, and often carried her little daughter, Jane, to spend the day with the old lady. Mrs. Benson and Colonel Hugh Mercer, "Virginia's Child of the Republic," were born the same day, and the same authority says, "that courteous old gentleman" of the Sentry Box, the son of General Hugh Mercer, never failed each year to pay his compliments and congratulations to her on that day. Jane Benson made her will in 1846, but it was not recorded until 1858. She left her property, consisting mainly of a house and lot corner George and Water Streets, with "brick building thereon," to her two daughters, Isabella Y. and Mary Jane Benson. The older citizens of Fredericksburg remember with pleasure Miss Bella and Miss Mary Benson.

BERRY: In memory of Our Mother, Mary Hill, wife of Thomas I. Berry. Died June 8th, 1865 in the 58th year of her age.

BERRY: In memory of Our Father, Thomas I. Berry. Died March 27th, 1859, in the 52nd year of his age.

Thomas I. Berry was an enthusiastic member of Lodge No. 4. He was a lover of horses, and his livery stables were often the means of conveyance to remote distances. His children were John K., Thomas Benton, Holder, Mary, who married William J. Moon, a well-known jeweler here in the latter part of the last century, and Alice Berry, who became Mrs. Winder. Mr. and Mrs. Moon, with their big family of girls and boys, occupied the Mary Washington house before it became the property of the Association for the Preservation of Virginia Antiquities. It is through the agency of Mr. Moon's careful custody that several Washington relics are still extant.

BLAIR: Here lies the body of David Blair, a native of Angus Shire, North Britain. Born Feby. 18th, 1710, and departed this life June 29th, 1801. An honest man's the noblest work of God.

This tried and trusted old Scotchman, David Blair, was secretary of the Fredericksburg Lodge of Masons. His name appears on an order authorizing the issuance of a charter for holding a Lodge in Gloucester, October 10, 1770. His will was probated in 1801. In it he says: "This 31st day of January in the year of our Lord 1800 being a remarkably snowy day, I can not get out of doors. I therefore sit down to make my last will and testament . . . wish my body to be buried alongside of my daughter, Isabella, in the Mason's burying-ground . . . I appoint my trusty and well-beloved friends, Benjamin Day, Daniel Grinnan, Robert Walker and Anthony Buck my Executors . . ."

James Blair, brother of David, must also be sleeping nearby, though there is no stone to tell his story. In his will written April 14, 1800, "my birthday," he said: "It is my wish to be buried as a Mason in the Mason's burying-ground, and this request is particular, because at this moment I am not conscious of having committed a single act to prevent it. My beloved brother knows where I have a child lying, I wish to be as near as possible to her, and one of his in the same grounds." He names his wife, Helen, and children, Janet, Helen, Barbary, and leaves a special legacy of Hume's *History of England*, his Mason's medal, and a Bible "I brought to this country with me," to his son, Andrew William Blair. He also mentions David and James Upton Blair, his nephews, and James Shepherd, "son of my good and worthy father-in-law." James Blair must have married Helen, the daughter of Andrew Shepherd, of Orange. It may be that once upon a time the name, James Blair, was conspicuous on the reticent old red sandstone slab which still stands so stoutly nearby! In Hayden's Genealogies, David and James Blair are mentioned as "Scotch importing merchants of Fredericksburg."

BLAYDES: In memory of Stephen J. Blaydes, Merchant. Died April 29th, 1858. Aged 69 years.

Stephen Blaydes, in his will probated in 1858, left most of his property to his sister, Elizabeth B. Crist, and to his nieces and nephews. The names Edenton, Acors, Dickinson, etc., appear, and John H. Wallace and John M. Herndon were his executors. He was a widely known merchant of this city, and had by "years of untiring industry accumulated quite a fortune."

BROCK: Sacred to the memory of my brother, Cadwallader Brock. Aged 39. January 17, 1843. Lord remember me when thou comest into Thy Kingdom.

Cadwallader Brock's mother was Ann Chew Brock,. of Spotsylvania, and Catherine Chew Brock, Caroline Chew Stanard, and John Chew were among his many uncles and aunts. In the will of John Chew (probated July 2, 1838), who is buried in close proximity, he releases his nephew, C. W. Brock, "from all the claims I have against him." He was also a beneficiary of Catherine Chew Brock. The little marble shaft to his memory, surmounted by a small cross of beautiful proportions, is one of the pleasing ones in the cemetery. One seems to read a note of peculiar pathos in the little information to be found about this comparatively young man.

BROWN: Inscribed by William B. Brown to the memory of his affectionate wife, Helen Herriot Brown, who was born at Edinburgh in Scotland, and died in Fredericksburg the 17th of February, 1810, aged 34 years.

The above named William Boyd Brown a native of Ayrshire in Scotland, Died December 12th, 1812. Aged 36 years.

Tho remote from his kindred and home, his

strict integrity, independent mind and affability of manners gained him general esteem.

William Brown bequeathed his property, according to his will probated 1812, to his sister-in-law, Margaret, Mrs. Archibald Duff of Edinburgh in Scotland, to Mr. James Dixon, of Standardsville, and to a nephew, William Wright, of Ayrshire, Scotland. Among his other legacies are his watch and money to William D. Payne, his set of Mavois *Voyages and Travels*, and the works of Burns, to Mr. George Cox, to Mrs. Ware the fringeloom, "formerly belonging to my wife," and another bequest to James Dixon is, "my dog Hector, my gun, and shooting apparatus." William McKechney, Reuben T. Thom, F. J. Nock, and Charles L. Carter were witnesses to his will.

BUCK: In memory of Andrew S., son of Anthony and Mary Buck, who departed this life on the 14th Day of October, 1828. Aged 26 years. He was a dutiful and affectionate son, and died much lamented by all who knew him. This stone is placed over his remains in testimony of affectionate and fraternal regard by his brother John.

BUCK: Departed this life 12th November 1842, Anthony Buck, Esqr.   Aged 76 years.   A native of Whiteburgh in England.   Enjoyed the respect and esteem of all who knew him.   Touching this spot lie the remains of his wife, Mrs. Mary Buck, who died the 28th of August, 1842. Aged 60 years.   Deeply lamented their children have placed this tomb as an affectionate tribute to their memory.

The Bucks are ancestors of some of the most substantial citizens of Fredericksburg today.   The Masonic apron of Anthony Buck is among the cherished relics of Fredericksburg Lodge, No. 4.   It is more simple in its design than many of the others, being plain white satin with blue ribbon quillings.   In his will made in November, 1842, he mentions his daughters, Sarah G. Buck, Elizabeth S. Buck, Mary Miller Smith, wife of Dr. Austin Smith; Margaret Smith, the wife of John H. Smith; Harriet S. Patton, wife of Dr. William F. Patton; daughter-in-law, Mary Conway Buck, and son, John.   The latter, with John H. Smith and "my friend, Hugh Patton," were his executors.

Mrs. Mary Buck was the daughter of Andrew Shepherd, of Orange.

Buck: In memory of John Buck Who was beloved by all. Died November 28th, 1851. Aged 54 years.

John Buck was a pew owner in St. George's Church in 1832. His wife was Mary Conway Buck. She long survived her husband. They were the parents of the late Mrs. Medora Buck Little, who for years lived with her family at their home on Hanover Street.

———

Callender: Memento Mori! Here lies buried the body of Eliezer Callender of Boston in New England, who departed this life the 9th of November in the year of our Lord 1792 in the 53rd year of his age.

This is one of the oldest stones in the cemetery. One wonders if he was not connected in some way with John Callender, clerk in the Parish of St. George at that time. His property was appraised in January, 1793, "under order of the Worshipfull Court of Hustings for the City of Fredericksburg," and though figures tell in plain terms that he could not command much wealth, his property sounds most alluring in these days of the search for such things. His "large mahogany dining table, large looking glass, silver Milk Pott, Brass Handirons, Shovell and Tongs, Dutch oven, Scotch carpets, chests of drawers, table spoons, 1 soup ladle," . . . etc., to which were added a cow, and a "Park Phaeton";—these were some of his treasures. F. Thornton, Jr., Gust. B. Wallace, and John Frazer were his appraisers. Campbell's *History of Virginia* records the name, "Eliezer Callender," who was a naval captain in the War of the Revolution. Possibly this was the same man. His being from Boston seems to strengthen the supposition. At the Library of Congress there is a little pamphlet (1911) on the Callender family which tells that members of the family have attained distinction in Boston. One Eleazer Callender was grandson of Michael Callender, who came to this country with Governor Winthrop in 1630. This Eliezer Callender was "Overseer of the Poor" for many years (which seemed an unusually honorable position) and was one of the original members of the Society of the Cincinnati.

CAMPBELL: In memory of Mrs. Christian Campbell, late of Williamsburgh, Relict of Doctor Ebenezer Campbell, formerly of Petersburgh, who departed this life 25th March, 1792, in the 70th year of her age. She was humane, generous, and kind, an affectionate and indulgent parent, warm in her attachments, Sincere in her pro-

Carmichael home on Hanover Street. To the right is "the office" where the Doctors Carmichael practiced their profession.

fessions, An enemy to oppression, A friend to the distressed, The means whose relief she generously exercised and promoted. She lived respectably beyond the usual period of mortality, Till life's taper gradually declined, and died universally beloved as universally lamented.

CARMICHAEL: Erected to the memory of Dr. James Carmichael By his family. Born in Glasgow, Scotland on the 30th of November 1771 and died in Fredericksburg on the 14th June, 1831, in the 60th year of his life. James Daniel, Edward Smith, Peter Gordon, and Harriet Randolph, infant children of James and Elizabeth Carmichael. Elizabeth Hackley, Francis Taylor, Wil'l Henry Taylor, infant children of Edward H. and Sarah L. Carmichael.

Dr. James Carmichael, his two sons, his grandson, and his great-grandson, furnish still another proof of our debt to Scotland. These five doctors have added lustre to the medical profession in this community. The name is conspicuous among the members of St. George's Church in 1816 and thereafter. He mentions in his will his wife, who was Elizabeth Hackley; his sons, Richard, George and Edward, and his daughters, Ann, Ellen and Janet, and the latter's husband, Charles Goodwin. His executors were William I. Roberts and Thomas Seddon.

His son, Edward, married Sarah Taylor, George French married Mary Carter Wellford, and Richard married Virginia Bernard. His daughter, Ann, was the wife of Mr. Hart, and Eleanor never married.

CARTER: Dr. Charles Landon Carter. Born May 21st, 1774. Died September 21st, 1832. Mary Randolph Carter. Born Oct. 19th, 1780. Died Oct. 1st, 1851.

In a Fredericksburg paper of 1832 is found a very beautiful tribute to the character of Dr. Carter. If the charming old miniatures of the old days tell the truth, he is well deserving of the tribute, for the features portrayed in his miniature, now in possession of relatives, seem to verify the statement that "he was possessed of great decision and firmness of character . . . was always governed by the purest principles of philanthropy . . ." After his classical school days in Fredericksburg, he studied medicine in Philadelphia. It was during that trying period when the dread disease, yellow fever, was raging, and Dr. Carter remained firm at his post. After his graduation in Philadelphia, "he was honored with the regard and confidence of George Washington and Thomas Jefferson," and to have those eminent citizens among his patrons and friends was strong evidence of his high moral worth. He, at one time, went to China, and was surgeon and physician on ship-board. Returning to his native town, he married Mary Randolph Thornton, daughter of the widow, Mrs. John Thornton, who afterwards married Dr. Robert Wellford, the first of the name to settle in Virginia.

Records show that Dr. Carter was vestryman in St. George's Church in the early years of the nineteenth century, but when he died the funeral services were held in the Presbyterian Church, "of which he was a member." He was a son of Charles Carter, and was twice mayor of Fredericksburg. Mrs. Mary Randolph Carter "went about doing good, and preaching righteousness by the prevailing eloquence of a pious example . . ."

CARTER: Sacred to the memory of Maleleel W. Carter. Born March 12th, 1798. Died January 20th, 1849. A tribute of his bereaved wife . . . worth of the best of husbands, and a monument of exalted regard for his character as a man of Justice and Honor. Grant him Oh Lord eternal rest in the realms of Perfect Light and Bliss.

Farewell, but not a long farewell
In heaven may I appear

The trials of my faith to tell
In thy transported ear
And sing with thee the eternal strain
Worthy the lamb that once was slain.

The name Maleleell W. Carter and wife, Harriet L. Carter, appear on an old deed dated 1846, in which there is a transfer of property, slaves and land, from them to Hugh M. Patton.

———

CHEW: Sacred to the memory of Elizabeth Chew, the worthy consort of John Chew, deceased, who departed this life May 21st, 1806. Aged 47 years.

———

CHEW: Sacred to the memory of John Chew who departed this life Feb. 12th, 1806, in the 53rd year of his age.

John Chew, Jr., was appointed on the 6th of August, 1787, clerk of the Hustings Court of Fredericksburg, and held the position until his death in 1806. This was the first appointment to this office in the Chew family and a remarkable feature is that it was held successively by four generations of the same family—from 1787 to 1886. John Chew was a vestryman in St. George's Church in 1803. In his will made in 1805 he mentions his wife, Elizabeth; his son, Robert S., and daughter, Mary Beverly Barton. He leaves his grandson, John James Chew, "my gold watch and chain and gold seal in token of my love and affection for him."

CHEW: John Chew. Born 1773. Died 1837. Aged 65 years.

John Chew who sleeps beneath this flat stone is a brother of Caroline M. Chew Stanard, whose last resaing place adjoins his on the south. His nephew, Cadwallader Brock, is contiguous on the north. Possibly John Chew never married, as no sign of wife or children appear in his will made October 11, 1837. He mentions his sisters, Philadelphia C. Waller, Ann Brock, Elizabeth Cammack, Mary Chew, Caroline M. Stanard, and brothers, Thomas and Robert Chew, and Beverley Chew, of New Orleans, and Cadwallader W. Brock, his nephew. Among the interesting items which he leaves are "my silver cup, my gold watch and chain, my double barrelled gun, & my silver-mounted pistols in a mahogany case." He is most solicitous that his executors pay to Fredericksburg Lodge, No. 4, "the sum of nearly $400 . . . which they deposited with me for safe keeping . . . the exact sum will appear on the books of the Lodge." To Louisa A. Skymanski and Maria B. Peacock he leaves $500 each to help educate their children.

CHEW: Here lies the body of Robert B. Chew, who departed this life the 30th day of December, 1791. Aged 37 years.

Robert Beverley Chew was a brother of John Chew, who was the first of the Chews appointed clerk of the Hustings Court. His will was proved February 7, 1792. Legatees were his nephew, Robert S. Chew; his nieces, Polly and Elizabeth Chew, and his brothers, Beverley, John, and Joseph are also mentioned.

CHEW: Sacred to the memory of Robert Smith Chew, who departed this life on the 2nd day of November in the year 1826 in the 47th year of his age.

Go, just in word, in every thought sincere
Who knows no wish but what the world might
    hear.
Of gentlest manner, unaffected mind,
Lover of peace and friend of human kind
Composed in sufferings, and in joy sedate
Good without noise, without pretension great.
Go live! for heaven's eternal year is thine
Go! and exalt thy moral to devine.

Robert S. Chew succeeded his father, John

Chew, in the office of clerk of the Hustings Court. (This was later Corporation Court.) He was a vestryman in St. George's Church in 1813. In his will made October 17, 1821, he leaves the greater part of his estate to his wife, Elisa, who was the daughter of Dr. George French. He wants his sister, Elizabeth French, the widow of Dr. James French, to have the annual rent from "the Island, which I purchased from John Mortimer." John was the son of Dr. Charles Mortimer who previously owned the "Island Plantation." (This is still a spot of wild and rugged beauty, and has, and will ever have, that subtle and inescapable atmosphere of romance which adds to its magnetism.) Robert Chew also leaves to his daughter, Ann Elisa, "the house now occupied by Samuel Howison," and other property to his three sons, John James, George French, and Robert Smith Chew.

———

COLEMAN: In memory of Charles Johnston, son of John W. and Eliza W. Coleman. Born March 5th, 1813. Died April 8th, 1850.

The father of Charles Johnston, who was John W. Coleman, was a member of Lodge No. 4 about this time.

———

COONS: In memory of Willie Dillard, son of Dr. A. J. and Fannie M. Coons. Died May 23rd, 1850. Aged 1 year, 3 months and 15 days. I shall go to him but he shall not return to me.

CRUMP: In memory of Robert Lewis, the only child of Robert H. and S. M. Crump, who departed this life on the 21st November, 1835. Aged 2 years and 26 days.

> As the sweet flower that scents the morn
> But withers in the rising day
> Thus lovely was this infant's dawn
> Thus swiftly fled its life away.
> It died to sin, it died to cares
> But for a moment felt the rod
> Oh mourner such the Lord declares
> Such are the children of our God.

Robert Lewis Crump was the little grandson of Robert T. and Mary Ellis. His mother was Selena Ellis Crump.

DAY: In memory of Benjamin Day. Born in London 24th September, 1752 and died in Fredericksburg 16th of February, 1821. He removed to this country early in life and took an active part in the Revolution, having served with credit as an officer of the American Army. A great portion of his time since has been devoted to the public in discharging the duties of magistrate, in which he was uncommonly zealous and useful. The Male Charity School of Fredericksburg is chiefly indebted to him for its origin in 1795, and for its prosperity to his unremitted attention in the principal management of its concerns, over which he presided until the time of his death.

The history of Fredericksburg's past would be incomplete without a recital of the activities of Major Benjamin Day. He was twice mayor of the town, and warden and vestryman in St. George's Church for a long period of time. His inclination and his means made him a real philanthropist. An extract from his will made in 1818 is interesting: ". . . I request that my body be interred in the Burial Ground of my much respected friends, the Masons of Lodge No. 4 . . . My servants Betsy and Nat to be immediately emancipated after my death . . . To my very dear children Sarah Nelson, Christiana Yates Benson, & Maria Russell Day," he leaves property.

"To John Mundell my composed microscope, to John Scott my globes, and to my friend William Lovell my gold headed cane. Having originated the Charity School of Fredericksburg I wished to have extended my patronage of it after my death, but considerations, known to some of my particular friends, prevent it." His sons-in-law, Thomas

Cary Nelson and John B. Benson, with John Mundell, John Scott, William I. Roberts and John Metcalfe, are witnesses or executors. He was adjutant Second Virginia Regiment in 1777. He is mentioned in the *Virginia Historical Magazine*, volume xxv, as a "commercial agent." He was an enthusiastic Mason, and was one of the five Grand Masters for the Grand Lodge of Virginia, furnished by Fredericksburg Lodge, having been elected to that office November 27, 1797. Captain S. J. Quinn, in his *History of Fredericksburg Lodge* (1890) says: "Some few of our citizens remember Major Day with his ruffled shirt, knee breeches, and powdered cue, . . ."

Because of its interest, the following is quoted in full from the *Richmond Enquirer* of February 24, 1821:

"Another soldier of the Revolution is numbered with the dead!!

"Departed this life on Friday evening, the 16th instant, in the 69th year of his age. Major Benjamin Day, one of our oldest, most valued, and most respectable fellow-citizens.

"His constitution was always delicate, but by great temperance in his mode of living, and much regularity in steady and correct habits, for which he was very remarkable, he attained the good old age to which he lived, and his death is more ascribable to a long and gradual decay of the functions of life than to any particular complaint or disease. Major Day was a zealous advocate for the rights of his adopted country, during the Revolutionary War, and served as aide de camp to General Woodford and Lord Stirling in that memorable struggle which gave independence to our country; and from those days, 'which tried men's souls,' to that which closed his mortal course, he was the American patriot in heart and in principle.

"After the revolution he was for some years engaged in mercantile pursuits and confidential agencies connected with that business."—*Fredericksburg Herald.*

DAY: In memory of Ebenezer, the beloved wife of Benjamin Day, who departed this life Nov. 3rd, 1804, in the 51st year of her age. A Tender parent, an affectionate wife, just in every relative of life, kind, gentle, candid, generous and sincere, A friend to virtue and to virtue dear. Thus has she lived, lamented has she died Firm in her trust,—In God alone relied.

DIMMOCK: Sacred to the memory of Mary Lee Dimmock, Daughter of Charles and Henrietta Dimmock. Born 14th Nov., 1834. Died 14th August, 1837.

The father of Mary Lee Dimmock was a warm personal friend of General Robert E. Lee, and in the War Between the States was one of his brigadier-generals. An oil painting of General Dimmock, by W. G. Brown, hangs in the Virginia State Library. He held the office of chief of ordnance of the State of Virginia, having been appointed by Governor Letcher. He was a native of Massachusetts and graduated from West Point in 1821.

The mother of Mary Lee Dimmock was Henrietta Johnston.

DIXON: In memory of James Dixon, a native of Castle
Douglas, Scotland, who died in this town on the
20th of December, 1833, aged 57 years.

> Know thou O stranger of the fame
> Of this much lov'd, much valu'd name
> For none that knew him need be told
> A warmer heart Death ne'er made cold.
>
> **Burns.**

James Dixon must have been an attorney. His name is conspicuous on many of the old deeds and legal documents. He, too, was probably an old bachelor, and as a solace (if one can read correctly by the dim light shed upon his activities) he became absorbed in the sports of the day. A friend left him all his shooting apparatus, with his good dog "Hector" thrown in, and he owned one-third of the sailing vessel, "Sarah Ann, with all her tackle, apparel, and appurtenances."

DRUMMOND: Beneath this stone rest the mortal remains of Ann Fox Drummond Æ 27. The domestic virtues dwelt with her, and the spirit of philanthropy. She breathed Peace and Goodwill towards all. On the 2nd of September, 1805, her Soul left its earthly Tenement to seek in the Mansions of Bliss, the Crown of Immortality, for Virtue shall burst the Fetters of the Tomb.

While Hope, the smiling Cherub whispers Peace,
And waves and points to scenes of endless joy,
Points to the Port where cares and Sorrows cease,
Where Bliss unbounded reigns without alloy.

DRUMMOND: To the memory of William Drummond, who departed this life October the 14th, 1804. Aged 39 years. This stone is erected by his widow as a frail testimonial of her affection.

William Drummond was an important man in the community. He seemed associated with Dr. George French in several land transactions. He was town alderman when Dr. French was mayor. He was also a trustee of the Fredericksburg Charity School. His main business must have been that of a merchant. In the *Virginia Herald* of 1799 he advertises extensively. He has "Madeira Wines (genuine London market) in pipes, hogsheads and Jr. casks, also old Sherry of Excellent Quality. Raisins in barrels, and Window Glass . . . will give money or bills for flour and tobacco." "Such a variety," one says. "Yes, and what a fight would be on, if the wet days of yore were to be introduced to an eighteenth amendment, strictly enforced!" Many were the wine merchants in Fredericksburg about that time.

———

ELLIS: Charles H. Ellis. Died September 15, 1856. Aged 31 years.

This was a son of Robert and Mary Ellis.

———

ELLIS: Eleanor B. Ellis. Born 1828. Died 1904. Blessed are the pure in heart, for they shall see God.

This is the latest interment in the cemetery. "Miss Ellen" was a daughter of Robert and Mary Ellis. She made her will

December 12, 1899, and left everything to her sister Virginia. Witnesses were Lelia R. Hart, Selena C. Hart and Irene McDowell.

ELLIS: Mary, wife of Robert Ellis. Died June 6th, 1863, in her 78th year.

Asleep in Jesus.

From the little that has been handed down to this generation, concerning this wife and mother, one feels certain Mary Ellis was a highly esteemed woman.

ELLIS: Sacred to the memory of Robert Lewis, the eldest son of Robert and Mary Ellis, who departed this life on the 22nd day of April A. D. 1833. Aged 18 years, 1 month and 16 days.

This son heard the instruction of his father, and forsook not the law of his mother.
Proverbs 1 ch. 8 v.

ELLIS: Our Father, Robert T. Ellis. Died January 21st, 1843. Aged 62 years.

Robert and Mary Ellis were the parents of those highly esteemed old ladies, Misses Ann, Virginia and Ellen Ellis, who occupied an apartment on Commerce Street in the infant days of the present century. Other daughters were Mrs. Robert Hart, Mrs. Green, and Mrs. Selena M. Crump. It is said that Robert Ellis was in the milling business on quite a large scale. He and his family lived for years in the house on the corner of Princess Ann and Hanover Streets, now the Forbes' home. It is thought by some that he built the house.

———

FRENCH: In memory of Dorothea B. French, daughter of George and Ann French, who departed this life the 2nd day of July, 1803. Aged 9 years and 4 months.

The father of this little girl was Dr. George French, a leading physician of Fredericksburg at that time. He served eight terms as mayor of the town between the years 1790 and 1815. Dr. French came over from Scotland with his nephew, Dr. James Carmichael. In 1805 he was appointed chairman of a committee to provide for the poor of the town. He died June 1, 1824, aged seventy-three years. The *Virginia Herald* says: "Dr. French was for more than forty years a most respectable and extensive practitioner of medicine in this place. His death is greatly lamented by a large circle of relatives and friends."

Ann French, the mother of Dorothea, was the daughter of John Benger, and great-niece of Sir Alexander Spotswood, the pioneer in so many and varied accomplishments, and Virginia's talented and most famous Governor—he who descended from the ancient Scottish family of Spottiswoode.

Among Dorothea's brothers was William M. French, who married Miss Barton, and they were the parents of the late Seth Barton French, of New York, formerly of Fredericksburg. Deserving causes in this town are still the beneficiaries of the generosity of Mr. French's family.

GALLAWAY: In memory of Robert Gallaway, a native of Glasgow in Scotland, who died the 1st day of August, 1794. Aged 53 years and 8 days.

> God hides his own within the grave
> In safe repose to ly
> Till shades of Sin & Death be gone
> & Glory deck the Skye.

Little could be learned of this native of Scotland who passed away before he reached old age. That kindly fellow-feeling engendered in those having the same nativity prevailed, without a doubt, in his day, and Robert Gallaway must have had many a kindly friend here.

A characteristic old deed, interesting, though brimful of useless repetition, records through the redundancy of words, that Robert Gallaway bought property on Main Street, "near to the warehouse commonly called Royston's . . .", from William McWilliams (the second mayor of Fredericksburg) and Dorothea Brayne McWilliams, his wife. He is to pay seventeen pounds and eight shillings on the 1st day of January 1790, ". . . and must cause to be erected, one good and substantial house of brick, or well framed of wood, two stories high, each story of the customary height, and divide the same into roomes, and furnish and compleat them in a good, neat and substantial manner, at his own proper costs and charges. . . ."

Witnesses

    Thos. Colson
    Elisha Hall
    William Wiatt

George French and Benj. Day witnessed the acknowledgment of Dorothea.

Robert Gallaway also purchased property from Colonel Fielding and Betty Washington Lewis.

GOODWIN: In memory of James Carmichael, son of
Charles and Janett G. Goodwin. He was born
on the 17th of September, 1823, and died on the
25th of July, 1830. Suffer little children to
come unto me, ... for of such is the kingdom
of Heaven.

This little boy was the grandson of Dr.
James Carmichael.

GOODWIN: Marla Margaret, the infant daughter of
William P. and Caroline Goodwin, departed this
life July 23rd, 1822. Aged 4 months and 8
days.

> Go sweet infant, early blest
> Called from pain to happiness.

The father of this baby, William P. Goodwin, was a member of the good old Goodwin
family, probably a brother of Arthur Goodwin, so long a banker in this town. In looking over old papers of debts and claims one
judges that he was a merchant here, and
possibly not a very successful one.

GOODWIN: Caroline, the beloved wife of W. P. Goodwin, with perfect resignation to the will of her
maker, departed this life Decr. 29th, 1824.
Aged 27 years, 9 months and 24 days.

Thy will be done O Lord.

There is no stone to William P. Goodwin, the husband of this young wife, but he may be resting near.

———

GOOLRICK: John Goolrick, a native of Sligo in Ireland. Died on the 17th ————, 1840, in the
———— year of his age. For 45 years he was
a resident of Virginia, the whole of which time
he was honourably, faithfully engaged in the
instruction of her youth.

This stone is badly mutilated and almost undecipherable. John Goolrick made his will May 11, 1839. He mentions his wife, Rose Goolrick, and to her sister, Mrs. Dunlevy, he leaves his silver watch. To his son, George, he leaves his house and lot on Main Street. He wishes his "body to be buried in the Masonic Burial Ground of Lodge No. 4 in the plainest white coffin, and to be attended with as little expense as decency will permit." The house in which he taught many of the representative youths of his day is still standing on lower Main Street, enlarged and much improved. His Masonic apron is preserved at the Fredericksburg Lodge, and is—unexpectedly—more ornate than many of the others. It is of heavy white satin, and most of the emblems known to Masonry are embroidered thereon.

———

GORDON: To the memory of Bazil Gordon, who was born near Kirkcudbright in Scotland on the 15th May 1768 and died at Falmouth, Virginia, on the 20th of April, 1847. Anna Campbell Gordon, wife of Bazil Gordon, Born September 14th, 1784. Died October 8th, 1867. To the memory of Susan, William, Virginia Fitzhugh & Agnes Somerville, children of Bazil and Annie C. Gordon, who died in their childhood.

Bazil Gordon came to Virginia in 1783. He and his brother, Samuel, engaged in business in Falmouth, and built up a splendid trade in tobacco, cotton and general merchandise, mainly with England. Armistead Gordon, in *Gordons of Virginia*, says: "He left to his heirs one of the largest fortunes in the state, accumulated by indefatigable industry and the strictest integrity. He was a man of enlarged benevolence and great mercantile sagacity, but with the simplicity and purity of a child." The will of Bazil Gordon is an interesting document. When one reads of his many and varied financial ventures, all of which seemed successful, of his care and thought in the selection of his beneficiaries, and of his minute provisions for every emergency, he realizes the judgment, the discriminating intelligence, and the business efficiency which characterized the man. William A. Knox (Jr.), Henry M. Knox, and R. C. L. Moncure were witnesses to his will. The first two were nephews of his wife, and the latter was afterwards judge on the supreme bench of the Virginia Court of Appeals for more than thirty years.

Anna Campbell Knox Gordon, the wife of Bazil Gordon, was the daughter of William and Susanna Fitzhugh Knox, of Windsor Lodge, Culpeper county. After the death of William Knox, his widow retired to her estate, Belmont, near Falmouth, so as to be near her children, several of whom had been married and lived nearby. Belmont still commands that magnificent vista up and down the Rappahannock River, and it has of late years been enlarged and beautified. Susanna Knox died here and is buried in the old graveyard in Falmouth.

With the property and the many other bequests Bazil Gordon left his wife, Anna Campbell, was the selection "of any twelve of my slaves," a rather different viewpoint from the question of help today. But though that question is so difficult now, it is far

South entrance to Belmont.

more satisfactory, from many angles, than it was in 1847. Mrs. Gordon died in Baltimore of paralysis.

The Gordon monument is one of the imposing ones in this cemetery. Besides the inscription, here are engraved the significent Scotch thistle and leaves. An hour-glass and the wings of time are on each side.

GORDON: Sacred to the memory of Jessie Somerville Gordon, daughter of Samuel and Susan K. Gordon who departed this life in August, 1822.

This was the grandchild of William and Susanna Knox, and daughter of Samuel and Susan Fitzhugh Knox Gordon, of Kenmore. This interment antedates by several years those at the Gordon burying-ground near Kenmore.

GORDON: To the memory of Mary Ellen, wife of Douglas H. Gordon and daughter of Colin Clarke, who was born the 16th September, 1822, and departed this life the 22nd of December, 1848, in the 27th year of her age. Hast thou the vigor of thy youth, an eye that beams delight, a heart untaught to sigh, yet fear; youth oft-times healthful and at ease, anticipates a day it never sees.

Mary Ellen Clarke Gordon, of Gloucester county, was the first wife of Douglas Hamilton Gordon, and a daughter-in-law of Bazil Gordon. She and her husband resided in Fredericksburg, where she died soon after the birth of a daughter, Ellen, afterwards Mrs. Wilson. Mr. Douglas Gordon was a prominent member of the Town Council and a vestryman in St. George's Church. He was a member of that very important committee meeting held with General Robert E. Lee at Snowden, November 20, 1862, shortly before the tragedy of the Battle of Fredericksburg. Soon after this the family removed to Baltimore, Md.

GREEN : In memory of Anna Green, who departed this life 10th August, 1804. Aged 28 years.

Sleep soft in dust, wait the Almighty's will,
Then rise unchanged and be an angel still.

Surely a beautiful tribute is implied in this inscription to the memory of Anna Green!

GREEN : To the memory of Jones Green of the County of Culpeper, who died on the 20th day of June, 1858, in the 64th year of his age.

Jones Green was the son of Captain James Green of the American Revolution, and his wife, Betsy Jones. He was the grandson of

Robert Green, who emigrated from Ireland in 1710, and who married Eleanor Dunn of Scotland. Jones Green married Susan Scott, of Fredericksburg. He named his country seat in Culpeper "Greenock" in compliment to the old home of his wife's father in Scotland. There are many descendants of this couple in this vicinity and elsewhere.

GREEN: To the memory of Susan E. M., wife of Jones Green, of Culpeper County, and eldest child of John and F. S. Scott, of Fredericksburg. Born on the 24th day of January, 1800. Died on the 5th day of December, 1844.

Blessed are the dead who die in the Lord.

Susan Elizabeth Margaret Scott Green was born at "Scotia," the old Scott home on Charles Street, which must have been in its day a charming residence.

GRIFFIN: To the memory of Mrs. Mary Griffin, wife of Major Thomas Griffin, of Yorktown, this slab is erected. She departed this life August 11th, 1852. Aet. 77.

Griffin! Yorktown! Truly this combination has the real flavor of Colonial days! The will of Major Thomas Griffin, of Yorktown, was probated in that historic town in 1836.

He mentions his wife, Mary Griffin, and five grandchildren. Mrs. Griffin was a sister or a sister-in-law of Louisa Griffin, the wife of Colonel Hugh Mercer, and lived for years at the Sentry Box. In her will, made here in 1850, she leaves legacies to "my dear sister, Mrs. Mercer," to the church at Yorktown and to the Charity School in Fredericksburg. One supposes that Mary Griffin married her cousin, as was often the case in those days. If she was a sister of Mrs. Louisa Griffin Mercer, she was closely related to that famous Cyrus Griffin who married Lady Christina Stuart, when a medical student in Scotland. Christina was a daughter of the Earl of Traquair. The tale of this attachment and subsequent elopement, and the violent opposition thereto, is indeed a romantic and interesting story.

GRINNAN: In memory of Cornelia Grinnan, daughter of Daniel and H. B. Grinnan. Born February 2nd, 1821. Died December 20th, 1864.

Rev. Horace Hayden says: "Cornelia Grinnan was a woman of unusual culture. Her well-stored, sparkling mind, her brilliant conversational powers and ready wit, made her sought after in every circle. She was a kinsman of the Duke of Argyle and a great favorite with the Duke and also the Duchess Dowager, whom she visited at Adencaple Castle. On this visit Queen Victoria honored her with a private reception, and she formed an intimate friendship with Lady Amelia Matilda Murray, maid of honor to the Queen."

———

GRINNAN: Daniel Grinnan. An elder in the Presbyterian Church. He is dead, but his memory still liveth, He is gone—but his example is here; And the lustre and fragrance it giveth
 Shall linger for many a year.

A tribute of respect and of affection to my husband and two sons, Walter and Daniel. O there is joy in the grief of the weeper:
 Whose loss may above be restored;
And sweet is the sleep of the sleeper
 Who rests in the name of the Lord.

Daniel Grinnan came to Fredericksburg from Culpeper when a boy, about 1792, and was employed by James Somerville, a wealthy merchant of the town. Later he became a partner in the firm, Murray, Grinnan & Mundell, who built up a large foreign and domestic trade. He died March 25, 1830. A tribute to him in one of the leading newspapers of the day has this paragraph: "... Few men have passed through life with a more unblemished reputation. ... His undoubted integrity, his intelligent and well cultivated mind . . . his open-hearted and generous benevolence . . . his unfeigned piety, will long be recollected by all who knew him . . ." In his will probated in 1830, he mentions "Presque Isle, my farm in Culpeper." This stout and still beautiful old brick mansion with its thick walls and hand carved woodwork was built in 1815. The huge brick stable, the slaves' quarters, the spring house and dairy house are all still here. A splendid herd of dairy cattle forms a part of the possessions of the present owner. John S. Wellford, Jeremiah Morton, and John Glassell were executors, and Robert Patton, James Carmichael, George F. Carmichael, and Samuel B. Wilson were witnesses to the will of Daniel Grinnan.

———

GRINNAN: Daniel Grinnan, Son of Daniel and Helen B. Grinnan. Aged 1 year and 4 months.

———

GRINNAN: In memory of Daniella M. Grinnan. Born Sept. 29th, 1830. Died Feb. 13th, 1888.

Daniella Morton was the daughter of Daniel and Helen Buchan Glassell Grinnan.

———

GRINNAN: In memory of my daughters Eliza and Helen Mary Grinnan. Died May 20th, 1846, June 11th, 1847. Their sun went down, Ere it yet was noon. Yet For them to die was gain.

These were daughters of Daniel and Helen B. Grinnan.

―――――――

GRINNAN: Our Mother, Helen B. Glassell, relict of Daniel Grinnan, of Fredericksburg. Died October 16th, 1853, in the 69th year of her age. Living the life of the righteous, Dying in the triumphs of the Gospel. (Her last words) All is well—all is well with me now and forever, and forever more.

Helen Buchan Glassell Grinnan, of Torthowald, Madison county (formerly Culpeper), was the daughter of Andrew Glassell, of Scotch ancestry. She married Daniel Grinnan, November 20, 1815. Her old home, Torthowald, was patterned after the old home in Scotland, and the workmen who erected it were brought over from that country.

―――――――

GRINNAN: In memory of Robert A. Grinnan. Born May 24th, 1817. Died October 19th, 1884.

Robert was the eldest child of Daniel and Helen Glassell Grinnan.

―――――――

GRINNAN: Walter Grinnan, Son of Daniel and Eliza R. Grinnan. Died July 1st, 1817. Aged 6 years and 8 months.

Walter Grinnan was the son of Daniel and his first wife, Eliza Richards Green Grinnan, daughter of Timothy Green.

HARROW: James D. Harrow. Born Dec. 15th, 1789. Died Aug. 22nd, 1851.

Mr. Harrow was for a time associated with Timothy Green in publishing the old *Virginia Herald*, and after that he and Jesse White carried on its affairs. James Harrow was the son of Gilbert Harrow, professor of mathematics in the old Fredericksburg Academy. It is said that the father was an unusually intelligent and cultured gentleman, and the son a most interesting man. Samuel Southard, of New Jersey, Secretary of the Navy under President Monroe, was his uncle by marriage, and it was at a handsome stag dinner here, given in his honor, that he (Senator Southard) was seized with apoplexy, and died shortly afterwards. This was soon after his resignation from the United States Senate, May 3, 1842. James Harrow was a member of the Presbyterian Church.

HART: Sacred to the memory of Harriet Hart, the beloved wife of John Hart, who departed this life on the 1st January, 1825, in the 29th year of her age.

And I heard a voice from Heaven saying unto me, write Blessed are the dead which die in the Lord, from henceforth, yea saith the Spirit that they may rest from their labours, and their works do follow them. Rev. XIV-13.

> Jesus can make a dying bed
> Feel soft as downy pillows are
> While on his breast, I lean my head
> And breathe my life out sweetly there.

HART: Sacred to the memory of John Hart, who departed this life January 8th, 1852. Aged 52 years.

The family of Hart seems extinct in this locality today. But this couple with their children, grandchildren and great-grandchildren ably represented for several generations the intelligence, the culture, the kindness and courtesy which were characteristics of the people of the town. Horace Hayden says that Harriet Hart was a daughter of Timothy Green, the pioneer editor.

HEATH: In memory of James Heath, who departed
this life at Snowden on the morning of the 3rd
of Dec., 1846, In the 84th year of his age.

James Heath was a man of "scholarly
tastes, and was possessed of a good deal of
property." He was related to the family of
Yeaman Smith, of Snowden, through the
Waddey family—Nancy Waddey having
married Robert Osborne, and Mary marry-
ing James Heath, his paternal ancestor. A
paragraph from an old letter from the late
Mrs. John L. Stansbury, of Snowden, daughter of Yeaman Smith, reads: "When I was
a child, about sixty years ago or more, I had
an old relative, a graduate of old William
and Mary before the Revolutionary War, a
resident in my father's family, who under-
took to teach me the dead languages . . ."
This was James Heath. He was a lawyer
by profession, but illness compelled him to
seek a retired life, and Snowden and his relatives attracted him. (Snowden is still a
lovely, restful, and attractive country seat.)
Mr. Heath seems to have taken a lively interest in Fredericksburg affairs, as his name
is often seen on various old business
documents.

*Recently restored apothecary shop of General Hugh Mercer, later the home of
David Henderson and his family.*

HENDERSON: In memory of David Henderson. Born
at Kirkaldy, Scotland, June 1st, 1754. Died at
Fredericksburg, Va., Jan. 28th, 1838.

————

HENDERSON: In memory of Mrs. Mildred Henderson,
wife of David Henderson, Senr., who departed
this life Feb. 26th, 1818. Aged 54 years. Near
her are interred William, Margaret, John, James,
and Charles, children of David and Mildred
Henderson, who died in their infancy, also their
son, Thomas Henderson, who died Dec. 28th,
1799. Aged 16 years.

There is a charming little house and "back
yard," with boxwood, stone steps, and ter-
races, on the corner of Main and Amelia
Streets, which—through the efforts of the
Citizens Guild of George Washington's boy-
hood home—has been lately brought back to
its original self. It is not alone a reminder
of Dr. Hugh Mercer and his apothecary shop
of Colonial days, but also of David Henderson, a prominent merchant of Fredericksburg, who must have occupied it in the
infancy of the eighteenth century. The locality was called as early as 1805 Henderson's corner, and retained that name until
comparatively recently. Some good fairy,
possessed with patriotism and alive to the
deathless deeds of General Hugh Mercer,
must keep continual guard over that little

corner. It is a fact that during the great fire of 1807 the high winds were so kind as to forbid the sparks to remain on that favored spot, while more substantial buildings, near and far, were entirely consumed.

David Henderson was an elder in the Presbyterian Church. His will, made in 1831 and proved in 1839, mentions his sons, David and Alexander; his daughters, Janet, Mary and Elizabeth, and his granddaughters, Mary Eleanor and Mildred. He recounts every item of his property and exonerates his sons from all charges on the books of David Henderson and Son. His son, Alexander, was his administrator, and James Dixon and John Hart witnesses to his will. A local writer calls his daughter, Janet, "the beautiful Miss Janet Henderson," and she is still handsome as Mrs. Spotswood Wellford, in the portrait which hangs at the home of one of her descendants. The will of his daughter, Elizabeth, was recorded in 1859. She gives to her sister, Mary Henderson Nelson, all her interest in "the House and Lot at the corner of Caroline [Main] and Amelia Streets, where I now reside," and finally, her niece, Mildred, daughter of her brother, Alexander, is to have it in possession. Mary Henderson married, about 1820, Armistead Nelson, of "The Dorrill," Hanover county.

The huge fireplace within was the instrument mainly responsible for the famous fried chicken, old Virginia ham and other dainties served by "Aunt Ginnie" to the family of David Henderson.

He was the youngest of seventeen children, and was the grandson of Secretary, afterwards Governor, Thomas Nelson, of Yorktown.

———

HILL: In memory of Ann Hill, who was born May 31st, 1802, and died July 30th, 1807. Aged 5 years, 1 month & 29 days.

> Sleep on sweet babe and take thy rest,
> God called thee home, He thought it best,
> For the dear babe no offence has given
> .... heaven.

HILL: In memory of John K. Hill. Born 20th May, 1807, and departed this life ———, 1808.

———

HILL: In memory of Sarah Ann Hill, The daughter of John and Ann Hill. Was born December 31st, 1810. Departed this life June 21st, 1813. Aged 2 years.

———

HOLBROOK: In memory of Sarah Evangeline, infant daughter of A. B. and R. A. Holbrook. Born Feb. 4th, 1851. Died March 26th, 1855.

———

JONES: In memory of William Jones, who died August 17th, 1812. Aged 46 years.

———

KALE: Albert Gallatin Kale Departed this life ———
         10th, 1826, Aged 8 months.

Sleep sweet innocence.

———

KALE: In memory of Anthony Kale, who was born
         in Chur Graubundten, Canton, Switzerland. De-
         parted this life August 7th, 1850, in the 60th
         year of his age.

Liberty and the pursuit of happiness in the new world attracted thither men from the lovely Swiss country also. In his will Anthony Kale leaves property to his wife, Catherine, to manage and use in any way that she thinks best, for the support of herself and children. He mentions his daughters, Maria Louisa (afterwards Mrs. J. T. Taylor), Mary E., Catherine C. and Julia A. (afterwards Mrs. Robert B. Alexander), and sons, William Edward, Richard Estes, and John Peter. Absolom Rowe, William Quisenberry, and John B. Alexander were witnesses to his will.

———

KALE: In memory of Catherine, wife of Anthony
         Kale, who departed this life Sept. 26th, 1859,
         in the 64th year of her age.

A Fredericksburg paper of that time says of Mrs. Kale: "... she had never attached

*From the lovely portrait of Ann Carmichael Kemeys
painted by J. P. Merrill.*

herself to any body of Christians, but she had 'pure and undefiled religion before God' . . . She was a kind neighbor and an affectionate mother . . ."

————

KEMEYS: The grave of Ann Fox Lindsey, wife of William Kemeys, of New York, and daughter of Dr. E. H. and Sarah L. Carmichael, who died December 30th, 1846, In the 27th year of her age.

This is Ann Carmichael! The foregoing is all that the big stone records of the daring and impetuous belle and beauty, Ann Carmichael Kemeys, whose winning face smiles down from above the miniatures, which lend their interest to the low, broad, white enamelled mantel at a lovely old-time home on Hanover Street, the residence of her father and grandfather, and still occupied by Carmichaels. Her sweet and sunny characteristics, her love of the initiative, her abounding charity and sympathy, her absorbing love affair, with its vital consequences, and her early death, combine to make the story of her life an interesting bit of Fredericksburg biography.

In her very youthful days she reciprocated the affections of, and fell romantically in love with young Shakespeare Caldwell—his name alone suggests a Romeo, an Anthony, an Orsino, or a Lorenzo—and it is said his personality was not surpassed by even those great heart-breaking characters. But alas! his father was an actor, and those days are not these days. Opposition won the day and she married another. To those familiar with her story, the flat stone to her memory, with its simple inscription, suggests a tragedy.

Incidentally Shakespeare Caldwell removed to Cincinnati, and the newspapers of a few years thereafter tell of his material prosperity, and of his marriage to Miss Breckenridge in Louisville, Ky., when ". . . the festivities were glorious . . . the wedding cake nine feet high . . . and the company was immense."

<hr>

KNOX: In memory of Elizabeth J. W. Knox, consort of W. A. Knox, who died on the 8th day of April, 1849, in the 24th year of her age. Blessed are the dead who die in the Lord. They shall be mine saith the Lord of Hosts in that day when I make up my jewels. Malachi, chap. III, v. 17.

Before her marriage Elizabeth Knox was Elizabeth Jennings, of Fauquier county. The husband of Elizabeth, William A. Knox (Jr.), must be sleeping nearby, as he requests in his will, probated in 1851, to be buried in the "Masonick Ground, as near my wife Elizabeth as possible, and I furthermore request my heirs to place a simple stone, head and foot over each . . ." He wants "all monies . . . to be equally divided between my brothers and sisters, or their heirs." He mentions sisters, Annie Bell Knox and Sarah Alexander Ball, and brothers, Simon Bolivar and Henry Morson, also William Knox Soutter.

William A. Knox was the second son of William A. Knox (Sr.), and grandson of William and Susannah Fitzhugh Knox. The father left among his possessions, "8 or 9 acres near Poplar Spring." This was the old home of William A. Knox, Jr. The house in which he lived is still standing. It is of white brick, substantially reinforced by heavy iron tie-rods, and though it has a distinctly dilapidated air today, its quaintness lends a charm.*

Mrs. Ann Somerville Knox Hayes, the daughter of William Knox's Uncle Thomas, occupied the old Hayes home on Main Street, which is still in possession of descendants. Its attractive white enameled woodwork and other features tell of the architecture of an-

---

* Since writing the above line this little house has changed ownership, and is being repaired and enlarged, and from present appearances it promises to retain its quaint charm.

other day. Mrs. Hayes, with her children, Mary Ann, Sarah Stuart, James and John, used to consider it a delightful frolic to be taken, together with "Mammy Abbey," out to Cousin Willie's to spend a long day.

KNOX: Sacred to the memory of Sarah Ann, Daughter of William A. & Sarah C. Knox, who departed this life June 7th, 1814. Aged 3 months and 13 days. The days of man are but as grass. For he flourisheth as a flower of the field, For as soon as the wind goeth over it, it is gone, and the place thereof shall know it no more.

KNOX: In memory of our mother, Sarah C. Knox, relict of William A. Knox, born February 27th, 1795. Died July 20th, 1845.

Sarah Casson Alexander Knox was the daughter of William and Sarah Casson Alexander, and granddaughter of Thomas and Sarah Bruce Casson. She was lineally descended from John Alexander, who emigrated to Virginia from Scotland and settled in Stafford county in 1660. She was also of the family of William Alexander, "Lord Sterling," a major-general in the American Revolution, to whom the Congress of the United States sent direct messages of thanks for his "judicious measures," and "meritorious exertions . . ." in the war for American independence. General Alexander died January 15, 1783.

Knox: Sacred to the memory of Susan Gordon, Daughter of William A. & Sarah C. Knox, who departed this life April 8th, 1817—Aged 5 years & 4 months—Thy short earthly pilgrimage is ended—Thou art sheltered from the storms of this vale of misery—Go happy soul to the bosom of thy Redeemer, who waits to receive thy gentle spirit—Go and with countless multitudes of Saints and angels—Join in Halleluias to the Lamb, Who liveth forever and ever—

Knox: Sacred to the memory of William A. Knox, who departed this life September 8th, 1831. Aged 42 years. I heard a voice from Heaven saying unto me, Write, Blessed are the dead who died in the Lord, from henceforth: Yea, saith the Spirit that they may rest from their labours, and their works do follow them.

The family of Knox is an interesting one. Tradition, which has been corroborated by painstaking research, declares that in the eleventh century one Uchter, Earl of Northumberland, married Elgiva, daughter of Ethelred II, King of England. They or their descendants settled in Scotland, and in fee simple or by marriage they became possessed of four baronies, or lordships within the Regality of Renfrew, viz.: Knox, Ranfurly, Craigends, and Griff Castle. One of the lords fixed his residence in the Barony of Knox, and, surnames coming into use about that time, he was known thereafter as Adamus de Knox. The story of William Knox of Renfrew, who married Janet Somerville of the same locality, and of their three sons who emigrated to America, is indeed a pleasing narrative. By the will of John Knox, merchant of Falmouth, Va., made in 1768, he leaves extensive lands in Stafford county to his three brothers, William of Windsor Lodge, Culpeper, Robert of Charles county, Md., and Alexander, "over the sea." Litigation between the three Knox brothers and the heirs of Peter Hedgman of the same county, in which were involved many acres of land, must have been a burdensome tax on the intelligence, faithfulness, and patience of William, who acted with "power of attorney." One wonders if the final decision was satisfactory to the brothers!

William A. Knox was an important man in this community in the early years of the nineteenth century. He was a son of William Knox and Susanna Stuart Fitzhugh Knox, the latter being a daughter of Thomas

Fitzhugh, of Bosco-Belle, a beautiful old estate in Stafford county, now destroyed by fire. One of the sisters of William A. Knox. Anna Campbell Knox, married Bazil Gordon, of Falmouth; another, Susan, married Samuel Gordon, afterwards of Kenmore, and a brother, Dr. Thomas Fitzhugh Knox, married a Miss Rieley, and this couple were the parents of that genial old gentleman, Thomas Fitzhugh Knox, who may be remembered by some of the older residents of the town. It was a granddaughter of William A. Knox, Emily Soutter Dix, the wife of Dr. Morgan Dix, rector of Trinity Church, N. Y., who published for her children in 1895 that charming biography, *Reminiscences of the Knox and Soutter Families.*

Mr. Knox was senior warden of St. George's Church at one time and vestryman in the year 1815. His will was made in 1828 and probated in 1831, leaving "all to my dear wife and children." Thomas Seddon, Philip Alexander, and brother, John S. Knox, were his executors, and Carter L. Stevenson, William I. Roberts, Arthur A. Morson, John Moncure, William C. Beale, and others were named as securities.

LECKIE: In memory of James Leckie, who departed
        this life November 17th, 1788. Aged 33 years.

The name Leckie is seen only occasionally
on the old records here.

———

LEGG: Here lies the body of Lucy Lee Legg, who
        departed this life on the 11th of May in the
        year of our Lord, 1787, and twenty-fourth of
        her age. What is the fairest Face, the Sweet-
        est Eve, a pretty Flower that Blossoms but to
        die. What is the Longest Life a fleeting Dream
        For three or three-score years are all the same.
        What are the Joys of Earth, a gilded land,
        But Virtue leads us to the throne of God.
        This stone was placed here by her afflicted
        Husband as a monument of his sincere affection.

Lucy Lee Legg was in all probability the
relict of John Legg who was a "vendue and
commission" merchant here in the old days.
He promised "strict attention to those who
will favor him with their commands." He
died here in April, 1799, and the *Virginia
Herald* says of Captain John Legg, that his
characteristics "made him dear to his family,
beloved by his friends, and respected by all
who knew him." In his will he leaves property to his children, Thomas, John, and Mary
Ann, and also his sister-in-law, Ann Taylor.
William Lovell, Dr. George French, William

Kenmore, whose far-famed frescoes have echoed with the boyish call of Robert Lewis.

Drummond and Robert Galloway were chosen as his executors. He desires to be buried by his "dear departed wife," but if that wish were granted, the stone to tell the fact was omitted, or else it has gone the way that many other of the stones have gone. In 1784 Captain Legg was appointed sergeant of the corporation with a salary of 1,200 pounds of tobacco. Thomas Legge was here sometime after his father's death, but he removed to Charleston, S. C., where he died in November, 1814.

LEITCH: Sacred to the memory of Miss Sarah Leitch. Born Oct. 15th, 1782. Died Nov. 16th, 1843. She was an exemplary member of the Baptist Church for more than 30 years, and could say with the Psalmist, Into thy hand I commit my spirit: thou hast redeemed me O Lord God of Truth. Psalm XXXI, v. 5.

Sarah Leitch was doubtless an aunt or a sister of Mrs. George Rowe. She left property to her niece, Mary Ann Rowe.

LEWIS: ——— of Robert Lewis, Esqr., who died January 17th, 1829. Aged about 60 years. In the various relations of life he was faithful, courteous and kind, and as chief magistrate of this corporation he received grace to execute

Justice and maintain Truth. The Friend of good Order and Religion, he died in the hope of a happy Immortality.

Touching this spot lie the remains of his wife, Mrs. J. W. Lewis, who died Novr. 29th, 1830. Aged 56 years, and of his son, Robt. T. Lewis, who died Oct. 9th, 1823. Aged 17 years.

Among the distinguished people who sleep in this old cemetery, few rank above Robert Lewis, son of Colonel Fielding Lewis and his wife, Betty Washington Lewis. Their stately and interesting old home, now well known as Kenmore, was then on the outskirts of the town. Now it is in the center of a residential district, and is in possession of the Kenmore Association. This charming old landmark of Colonial days, and its fascinating interior, with its mural frescoes, is the joy and pride, not only of the citizens of this community, but the multitudes interested in Washingtoniana. Colonel Robert Lewis was born at the home of his parents about the year 1769. He was the private secretary to General Washington, his uncle, and acted as escort to Mrs. Martha Washington when she went to New York to attend the first inauguration of her illustrious husband. He gives an interesting account of this trip in his diary. He served several terms as mayor of Fredericksburg, dying in office. He was many times elected vestryman and warden in St. George's Episcopal Church. In 1824, as chief magistrate of the town, he made the welcoming speech to the distinguished friend of America, and the personal friend of General Washington, that great Frenchman, the Marquis de Lafayette. This was the occasion of the second visit of the Marquis to this town. He was now an old man, but the tender recollections of the mother of Washington, of Washington himself, and of "his dear sister, your own respected parent," Betty Washington Lewis, was manifest. An extract from the will of Robert Lewis is interesting: "... I give to my daughter Judith C. McGuire my pew in the Episcopal Church. I give to my grandson Robert Lewis McGuire my gold watch, which belonged to his grandfather Fielding Lewis, with an earnest request that he will not part with it. . . . I give to my beloved wife Judith Walker . . . my entire estate . . . I give my ferry over the Rappahannock at the lower end of said town . . . to my affectionate, obedient, and much loved daughter, Betty Burnett Bassett . . ." He also makes provision for "my faithful old servant Patty Robinson . . ." Witnesses to his will were John L. Marye, William A. Knox, and E. H. Carmichael.

Miss Anne Carter relates that the "Presbyterian sisters" used to assemble at the time of the annual election for mayor and pray that Colonel Lewis would be re-elected, since if he were not he would remove with his family to their country residence. It is said that Mrs. Judith Lewis was a "tower of strength in the early days of the Presbyterian Church." She was a leader in their prayer and song services, and was the author of many of the hymns sung at the numerous women's meetings, generally held at the homes of members on Gunnery Green. Rev. William Henry Foote, in his *Sketches* pays Mrs. Lewis a beautiful tribute in his chapter on Fredericksburg. She was Judith Walker Browne, daughter of William Burnett Browne, of Elsing Green, and Judith Carter, of Cleve, and granddaughter of William Brown, of Salem, Mass., and Mary Burnett. The latter was a daughter of Governor William Burnett, of New York and of Massachusetts. Governor Burnett was a son of the famous Gilbert Burnett, Bishop of Salisbury or New Sarum, early in the eighteenth century. Judith and Robert Lewis were married in 1791.

Although that splendid patriot, Colonel Fielding Lewis, the father of Robert Lewis, contributed so generously and so wisely to the success of the American Revolution, his will, made October 19, 1781, and proved in January, 1782, records "50000 pounds Sterling (specie)," that is, his executors gave bond for that amount. "A right nice little nest-egg," says one.

This he leaves his "beloved wife Betty" and children, of whom Laurence, Robert, and Howell were minors. It is difficult to arrive at a correct interpretation of Fielding Lewis' will. Perhaps even his "loveing wife" and "son John" found it involved. But it is not hard to construe the fact that his desire is to provide definitely and generously for Betty as long as she lives, and then, "my son John." To him he leaves much property, but on condition that he pay his (Fielding's) debt of "1500 pounds with interest at six per cent from the day of my death." His extensive possessions in Frederick county and in Kentucky (located by Mr. Hancock Lee) were left to sons. An interesting item he leaves to John is the silver cup which was his mother's, "which has a race-horse engraved thereon." Colonel Fielding Lewis' first wife was Catherine Washington, and John was a son of this union.

Writers say it was the young boy, Robert Lewis, who in 1784 carried the message to his grandmother, Mary Ball Washington, that Lafayette had arrived and wanted to see her. She was working in her flower garden at her home on Charles Street.

LITTLEPAGE: Here lies the body of Lewis Littlepage, who was born in the County of Hanover, in the State of Virginia, on the 19th day of December, 1762, and departed this life in Fredericksburg on the 19th of July, 1802, Aged 39 years and 7 months. Honoured for many years with the esteem and confidence of the unfortunate Stanislaus Augustus, King of Poland, he held under that monarch, until he lost his throne, the most distinguished offices, among which was that of Ambassador to Russia. He was by him created the Knight of St. Stanislaus, chamberlain and confidential secretary in his cabinet, and acted as his special envoy in the most important occasions of talents, of military as well as civil, he served with credit as an officer of high rank in different arms. In private life he was charitable, generous, and just, and in the various public offices which he filled, he acted with uniform magnanimity, fidelity, and honor.

General Lewis Littlepage was the fourth in line of descent from Richard of New Kent county, who was the first of the name known in Virginia. This Richard was a vestryman in St. Peter's Parish in 1685. The antecedents of Lewis Littlepage were prominent people in the Colony of Virginia, and mar-

The stone to the memory of Sir Lewis Littlepage is in the foreground, and those to the Chews, James Somerville and the Knoxes are not far away.

The name of Robert Lewis is inscribed on this old stone. The red sandstone mausoleum of General John Minor is beyond, and the quaint roof of James Monroe's law office is seen in the distance.

ried generally into prominent families. His father, Colonel James Littlepage, also of New Kent, was the first clerk of Louisa county. He was elected to the House of Burgesses from Hanover in 1764. On account of charges brought against him by Nathaniel West Dandridge, a big man in the affairs of New Kent county, strenuous efforts were made to have him unseated. And combined with these efforts was the oratory of the already famous Patrick Henry, whom West employed as his attorney. But his innocence was obviously established, as their efforts to unseat him were futile. Lewis Littlepage was the first-born of two children of his father's second marriage, about 1760, to Elizabeth Lewis. (After his father's death his mother was married, 1774, to Major Lewis Holladay, of Spotsylvania county.)

When only seventeen years of age he became ambitious of a political career, and when the Hon. John Jay was, in 1779, appointed to represent the United States at the court of Spain, he took the young boy with him as his protégé. It may be said that from this time on the history of Continental Europe would be incomplete without a mention of General Lewis Littlepage. His varied and interesting career and his early death have been so often chronicled that it is unnecessary to repeat it here. "He moved in the first circles of Paris and Versailles and other European cities," and historians say that wherever he went, and whatever his mission, he acquitted himself with distinguished ability. At Cadiz he formed an intimate friendship with General Lafayette. At Gibraltar he met the Prince of Nassau, whom he accompanied to Constantinople, and with the Prince attended the Diet of 1784 at Grodno, Poland, where he met Stanislaus Augustus, king of that country, who was completely captivated with the spirit of the youth of twenty-two years. It was at that time that he offered him one of the highest offices of his court. An extract from a letter written by his majesty, the King of Poland, is of interest. It is written April 27, 1795, and addressed to "Mr. General Washington, President of the United States, . . . Your conduct in war and peace has inspired me for a long time with the desire of expressing to you the high esteem which I bear you. . . . Mr. Lewis Littlepage knows the persons and the courts of almost all the princes of Europe both by the journeys he has made and the commissions I have given him, and of which he has always distinguished himself with much intelligence and activity. . . . Since he is thinking of returning to America I strong-

ly desire that he may be able to find there
an agreeable and sure destiny . . . in the
midst of that nation which has known how
to win for itself such an opinion from the
inhabitants of the old Hemisphere that . . .
it serves them as a lesson and a model. It
is very sincerely that I avow myself, Mr.
President of the United States, Your very
affectionate

Stanislaus Auguste, King."

The last line of a letter from General Lafayette shows his appreciation of the man,
". . . Adieu my dear Littlepage. Reply to
my letter as soon as you can. . . . I need it,
and I still have more need of speaking to
you, of embracing you, of the tender friendship which my heart has given you for life.

Lafayette."

On his way back to Poland in 1785, after
a visit in Virginia, he writes this letter to his
half-brother: "Alexandria: Dear Sir: I have
just arrived here from General Washington's, and shall set out in tomorrow's stage.
I was highly pleased with my visit at Mt.
Vernon . . . I found General Washington
much less reserved in conversation than I
had been taught to expect, and was peculiar-
ly happy in having an opportunity of inform-

ing myself of many interesting features of the American war, which no one but the General could properly attest. . . . P. S. I have sent some excellent tobacco for my mother and my uncle Zachary . . ." Besides those characteristics which made him so popular at European courts, Littlepage must have had under that military coat so decorated with honors, a heart full of affection, for his mother in particular, and other relatives and friends. Letters still extant and his last will attest this. He counted among his intimates in this country such men as Washington, Thomas Jefferson, John Paul Jones and others.

His was a versatile brain. His poetic ability was also of no mean quality, and one wonders how his time and his inclination—considering the many European broils in which he was involved—could have been attuned to that accomplishment.

Did he not crowd several generations of important activities in a short period of time? Less than forty years! When one remembers his naturally weak constitution, and the pertinent paragraph in a letter shortly before his death, "God knows I am sick of European politics," his premature passing is not surprising.

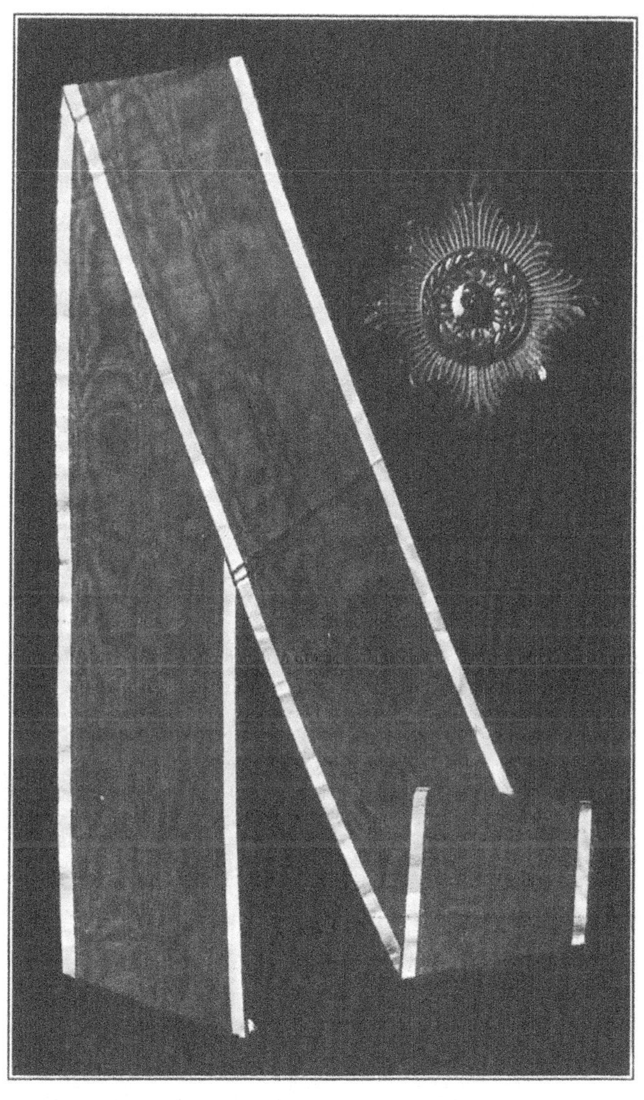

Court decorations of Sir Lewis Littlepage. The Star of the Order of St. Stanislaus—the badge of his knighthood—is brilliant with rubies. Now in possession of relatives.

LOMAX: In memory of Thomas Lunsford Lomax, son of Thomas Lunsford Lomax and Martha, his wife, afterwards the wife of W. I. Roberts, on 7th May, 1850.
Ann. etat 47.

Thomas Lunsford Lomax was the grandson of Mrs. Jane Johnston, and must have been a small boy in 1808, when her will was probated. She leaves all her "Green Brier Lands" to her grandson, Thomas Lunsford Lomax, because his mother (her daughter, Martha) is to "change her situation" by marriage. The mother, Martha, obviously married William I. Roberts, and her resting place is contiguous to that of her son. His father practiced his profession of attorney-at-law here in Fredericksburg.

LOVELL: In memory of Elizabeth Lovell. Born August 23rd, 1791. Died January 16th, 1795.

It is said that a family of Lovells once occupied Federal Hill, but moved to Fauquier. This little girl may have been of that family. William Lovell's name appears on many of the old deeds between 1797 and 1821.

MAURY: Sacred to the memory of Richard B. Maury,
who died on the morning of Nov. 25th, 1836.
Aged 44 years.

> The sweet remembrance of the just
> Shall flourish when he sleeps in dust.

Richard B. Maury was the son of Fontaine and Ellen Brooke Maury, and grandson of Rev. James Maury and Mary Walker Maury. He was a first cousin of Matthew Fontaine Maury, and the father of Rev. Magruder Maury, rector of St. George's Church from 1864 to 1871. He was an uncle of William Lewis Maury, who sleeps very near. Mrs. Ellen Maury, the widow of Richard B., taught school here after the death of her husband.

MAURY: Sacred to the memory of William Lewis
Maury, son of Lieutenant John M. Maury,
U. S. Navy, and Eliza, his wife, Born May 4th,
1818. Died Nov. 7th, 1838. Jesus Wept. A
mother weeps.

This simple expression, "A mother weeps," seems brimming with significance, and particularly so, if one acquaints himself with the facts of William Lewis Maury's short career, a life which, at the outset, gave every promise of fulfilling a large measure of worthwhile activities. His younger brother, afterwards General Dabney H. Maury, says: "He was a very handsome, attractive young fellow, and a great favorite." He died of heart disease when only twenty years old. His father was that capable sailor, John Minor Maury, flag captain of Commodore David Porter's fleet, who died in 1824, at thirty-one years of age. He married his cousin, Eliza Maury. That wonderful genius and Christian gentleman, Commodore Matthew Fontaine Maury, an uncle, became guardian of these little boys, and as is characteristic of his noble nature, no boys had ever a tenderer or more sympathetic parent. In Maury's *Recollections* he says that when he last visited St. Julien, the home of his relative, Judge Francis T. Brooke, a few miles below Fredericksburg, on the Tidewater Trail, he saw on the bark of an aspen tree, the big heart cut by his brother, with his initials and those of his young sweetheart, Mary Francis Thompson, carved thereon.

———

METCALFE: In memory of Alfred, son of J. & C. Metcalfe. Born 23rd Novr., 1824. Died 2nd May, 1826.

———

METCALFE: In memory of Ashton, son of Jno. & Cath. Metcalfe. Born 29th Jany., 1815. Died 8th Jany., 1818.

———

METCALFE: Sacred to the memory of Catherine Metcalfe, who was Catherine Johnson, b o r n in Louisa Co., and died in Fredericksburg, 11th August, 1843.   Aged 56 years.

For her to live was Christ, and to die was gain.

One cannot repress a feeling of keen regret when he enters that section of the cemetery where the name "Metcalfe" is so many times repeated. Seven little babies of John and Catherine Metcalfe sleep here, 1814-1826. In 1839 occurred the death in far away Africa of their daughter, that much loved pioneer in the mission field, Susan Metcalfe Savage. In 1840 another daughter, Louisa, just entering the portals of womanhood, is taken to "meet her God." Three years later the heart-broken wife and mother goes to her reward. Fourteen years elapse, and on March 19, 1857, the husband and father, full of years and responsibilities—but with such a measure of Christian faith and resignation as enabled him to cheerfully carry his cross—laid down his life.

Newspapers of that day have enthusiastic tributes to the worth of Mr. Metcalfe, although reticence on such subjects seemed characteristic of the papers of that day. An editorial in the *Virginia Herald*, entitled "A Good Citizen Gone," says: ". . . his was the heart ready to feel for other's sorrows, and his was the hand ready to relieve want. . . . In his every relation of life he commanded the respect and esteem of all. . . ." He was an active and zealous member of the vestry of St. George's Church, and an efficient officer in the Farmers Bank of Virginia, with which he had been connected since the day of its charter in 1812. The officers of the bank attended his funeral, "in a body," at the request of "A. Goodwin, Cashier." He was also a member of the Young Men's Christian Association. At a meeting of that organization in his memory "appropriate rearks were made by Dr. John S. Wellford, William S. Barton, John L. Marye, Jr., and William Slaughter, Esq." In his will, made two days before his death, Thomas F. Knox, William Brown, and William Warren, witnesses, he leaves property to his daughter, Lucy Hunton, also "all my silver and plate, and two sets of silver forks." The residue he leaves to his son, William Alfred. One feels indignant that no stone is there to record the fact that such a man lived. Nor is there a marker to his daughter, Lucy, who, the old church records tell, died in July, 1860, and was buried in the Masonic Cemetery. Mr. Metcalfe owned and occupied for many years the house on Princess Ann Street, which has also been for years the residence of Mr. Marion G. Willis and his family. The room on the west side, which John Metcalfe used for his office, is still here, but the big brick chimney equipped with that ingenious secret depository, where valuable papers could be safely housed, has now disappeared and its space used for more practical, if not as picturesque, purposes.

METCALFE: In memory of Charles Metcalfe, son of J. & C. Metcalfe. Born 4th Sept., 1816. Died 4th March, 1817.

METCALF: In memory of Eliza, daughter of Jno. & Cathe. Metcalfe. Born 21st May, 1813. Died 1st Augt., 1814.

METCALFE: In memory of John, son of J. & C. Metcalfe. Born 30th Novr., 1818. Died 23rd Decr., 1821.

METCALFE: Sacred to the memory of Mary Louisa, daughter of John and Catherine Metcalfe, who departed this life on the 1st day of February, 1840. Aged 18 years and 9 months.

Prepare to meet thy God.

At the home of Mr. Willis on Princess Ann Street, there is cut into a window pane on

Hazel Hill, the home of General John Minor.

the north side of the big room, once the Metcalfe parlor, the word "Louisa." One would
love to roll back the curtain of time and see
the situation which inspired this imprint!

METCALFE: In memory of Richard, son of J. & C.
Metcalfe. Born 28th Novr., 1822. Died 15th
Augt., 1824.

METCALFE: In memory of an infant daughter of
J. & C. Metcalfe. Born 15th Decr., 1817, and
died 3 days after.

MILNE: In memory of Margaret Milne, daughter of
Collin & Elizabeth Milne. Departed this life
(illegible).

MINOR: To our Father, General John Minor. Born
May 13th, 1761. Died at Richmond, June 8th,
1816. "He was as brave a man and as true a
patriot as ever lived."   Wm. Wirt.
Removed to this cemetery from Hazel Hill December 29, 1855. Blessed are the dead who
die in the Lord.

    Lucy To our Mother
Mrs. Mary Landon Minor. Born April 29,
1776. Died December 26, 1855. The righteous
shall be had in everlasting remembrance.

Though General John Minor, the third of
the name, had only attained his fifty-fifth

year at the time of his death, he crowded the activities and accomplishments of an octogenarian in that space of time. He was born at the home of his ancestors, Topping Castle, Caroline county, and became a soldier of the Revolution when a young boy. From that time until his death his life was full of well worth-while accomplishments. He was an eloquent lawyer, an intrepid soldier, and an engaging and warm-hearted citizen. In the War of 1812 he gained the title of general. He was a member of the Virginia House of Delegates, and it is said he took the initiative and introduced the first bill in the General Assembly for the emancipation and colonization of slaves. He was the uncle of the great scientist, Matthew F. Maury, and the intimate friend of James Monroe, and was a member of the electoral college which cast the Virginia vote at Monroe's first election to the presidency. General Minor made his will in 1814. Among the many items is this: "I, John Minor of Hazel Hill . . . give my wife Lucy Landon Minor . . . all my property," and appoints her sole executor. "But should she marry again I revoke this devise." One may read between the lines his all-absorbing wish, his unspoken request, that she should not re-marry, and it is satisfactory to note, though she lived many years

Magnolia trees, early apple blossoms and box-wood at Hazel Hill. The Stafford hill side, seen across the Rappahannock, was the theatre of the activities of the real little George Washington, and the native heath (if anywhere!) of the far-famed cherry tree.

after the passing of her brilliant husband, his wish was gratified. His first wife, who lived only a few months after her marriage, was Mary Berkeley, of Hanover county. His second wife was Lucy Landon Carter, daughter of Landon Carter, of Cleve, King George county. There were seven children of this union. General Minor's home was at beautiful Hazel Hill, at the lower end of Princess Ann Street, Fredericksburg, and though there have been many changes in ownership, it is still beautiful. The *Enquirer* of June 12, 1816, contains a beautiful tribute to him, by "one who knew General Minor well." At the time of his death he was in Richmond attending to some professional engagements, and after an illness of two days, he passed away "at his lodgings," at 8 o'clock P. M., Saturday, June 8, 1816.

NEWBY: In memory of Elizabeth Newby. Born Aug. 2nd, 1799. Died May, 1801.

Perhaps the father of this little girl was James Newby, one time proprietor of the Eagle Hotel, which stood, years ago, on Hanover Street, just above the side entrance to the present Maury Hotel. The name is also seen on stones in St. George's Church-yard.

OLIVIER: In memory of Elizabeth Olivier, who departed this life December 10th, 1793. Aged 25 years, and an infant aged 20 days.

The name Olivier appears often among the names of the old merchants of Fredericksburg.

———

PARKE: In memory of Ellenor Parke. Daughter of (broken off).

———

PARROTT: Jane Parrott. Daughter of R. & S. Parrott. Died July 14th, 1813. Aged 2 years & 3 months.

———

PARROT: In memory of Sarah Parrot, who departed this life June 25th, 180—. Aged 14 months and 17 days.

Robert and Sally Parrot were the parents of these two babies. They transferred lots on Caroline [Main] Street in 1809 to Colonel Hugh Mercer. They also owned lots on Dunmore Street,—the old Fredericksburg Academy property.

———

PATTON: George Weedon Patton, the infant son of Robert Patton and Ann Gordon, his wife, died on the 20th of October, 1801. Aged 7 months & 12 days.

You that ere lost an Angel Pity me.

This infant's mother was Ann Gordon Mercer Patton, daughter of General Hugh Mercer of Revolutionary fame, and his wife, Isabella Gordon. The latter's sister, Catherine, was the wife of General George Weedon, also of Revolutionary fame. The Gordon home was at the lower end of Main Street, long known as the "Sentry Box."

———

PATTON: Sacred to the memory of Harriet S. Patton, consort of Dr. Wm. F. Patton, U. S. N., who departed this life on the 7th day of December, 1849. Aged 41 years and 10 months.

Dr. Patton married Harriet Shepherd Buck, daughter of Anthony and Mary Buck, the progenitors of that family of Bucks. It is interesting to note that at the time of the death of Harriet Buck Patton, Dr. Patton, her husband, was of the United States Navy. She was a sister of Margaret, Elizabeth Hall, Sarah, William, and John Buck.

———

PATTON: Isabella Gordon Patton, the only daughter
of Robert Patton and Ann Gordon, his wife,
departed this life on the 3rd day of November,
1804. Aged 5 years, 1 month and 13 days.

Like blossomed trees o'erturned by vernal
storms
Lovely in death the beauteous ruin lay.

Isabella Gordon Patton was the granddaughter of General Hugh Mercer, killed at
the Battle of Princeton, and his wife, Isabella Gordon. Mrs. Ann Mercer Patton
donated the site for the Presbyterian Church
here, and many lineal descendants still occupy seats.

Rev. William H. Foote, in his sketch of
the Presbyterian congregation here, says:
". . . Next to Major Day sat the majestic
Patton, from his beautiful residence near the
Falls [White Plains]. . . . Mercer's daughter
was as frail as her husband was majestic . . ."

PATTON: Dr. W. F. Patton, C. S. N.

Dr. William Fairlie Patton was another
son of Robert and Ann Mercer Patton, and
grandson of General Hugh Mercer. The will
of Dr. Patton's mother mentions "My son at
sea." Dr. Patton died July 8, 1884, aged 83

The stone steps lead to the flower garden on the terrace at the Hugh Mercer Apothecary Shop.

years. He was of the Confederate States Navy.

The following is taken from the *Virginia Star* of July 12, 1884: "Death of a Former Citizen.—Dr. William F. Patton, formerly a citizen of this place, died at the residence of his son-in-law, General John R. Cooke, in Richmond, last Tuesday. Before the war he was surgeon in the U. S. service, and resigned his position at the breaking out of the war, and returned to his native state. He was a brother of Mrs. John James Chew, and uncle to Colonel Robert S. Chew. . . ."

Dr. Patton was brought here for interment and his funeral services were held in St. George's Episcopal Church. Of his children, Mary, who married Richard H. Catlett, of Staunton, and Anthony, who married Virginia Bernard Coakley, were twins. Nannie married General John Rogers Cooke and Fairlie Preston married Winnie T. Branham.

———

PATTON: Sacred to the memory of Wm. Fairlie, third son of Wm. F. and Harriet S. Patton, who died May 26th, 1847. Aged 6 years.

———

PEACOCK: Sacred to the memory of Hannah Peacock, who departed this life on the 29th day of June, 1818, in the 57th year of her age.

> partner of my breast . . . . yet
> remembering that the parting . . . .

It is said that when Rev. S. B. Wilson first established the Presbyterian Church here in 1806, the room was filled with Episcopalians, and among the names mentioned are Peacock, Chew, Mrs. Robert Lewis, Patton, and others.

PEACOCK: In memory of Maria Peacock, who departed this life the 15th June, 1798. Aged 2 years . . . .

RICHARDSON: Sacred to the memory of Ellen L. Richardson, third daughter of Mr. Thomas Richardson, of Richmond, who departed this life on the 8th day of August, 1821, at the residence of Doctor James Carmichael, in the 17th year of her age, deeply lamented by all who knew her.

> Peace to your ashes dear girl.

The father of Ellen Richardson died in Richmond in December, 1831. He was for many years a resident of that city.

Roberts: In this spot are deposited the mortal remains of Mrs. Martha Roberts, second wife
of William I. Roberts, of this town. She departed this life on Monday, December 11th,
1829, in the 48th year of her age.

She was all that cheered and sweetened life,
The tender mother, daughter, friend and wife.

Before her marriage to William I. Roberts
Mrs. Martha Roberts was Mrs. Martha
Lomax, the daughter of Mrs. Jane Johnston
and mother of Thomas Lunsford Lomax.
William I. Roberts was "cashier of the office
of Discount and Deposits of the Bank of
Virginia." If one can judge by the number
of times his name appears on legal papers,
and the various tributes paid to his integrity
and faithfulness, he was an important man
in this locality. His will, proved in 1842,
leaves his son, John H. Roberts, his beneficiary and executor. If he rests beside his
wife, there is no stone to mark his memory.

Roberts: Sacred to the memory of Mrs. Isabella
Roberts, who exchanged an earthly for a ce-
lestial abode on the 12th November, 1807, aged
33 years. She was a native of Scotland. While
living was a most exemplary pattern of piety
and virtue, and died a sincere and good christian.

A chatty old manuscript in the possession
of Mrs. V. M. Fleming is authority for say-

ing that "Mrs. Roberts" was the victim of the great conflagration which devastated the town in the fall of 1807. It originated at the residence of Mr. Larkin Stanard (where the Shepherd house now stands) and spread with great rapidity. That part of the town was at the time almost depopulated, all, except the incapacitated, attending the "Fall Races" in another section of the town.

The Bank of Virginia, which stood on Water Street, the site now occupied by the colored Baptists, was the second house to catch and was entirely consumed. Mr. Roberts was cashier of the bank, and Mrs. Roberts with her little new-born baby was carried from her living-rooms into the garden. Her feeble strength would not permit her recovery from this shock, and she passed away within a month thereafter.

ROSE: In memory of Jane Lawson Rose, the second daughter of Alex. F. and Mildred Rose, who departed this life the 20th of November, 1817.

Bereaved till Life can charm no more,
And mourn'd till pity's self be dead.

Alexander F. Rose, the father of this child, was the ancestor of the Roses of Falmouth and Fredericksburg. He was a vestryman in St. George's Church in 1814, and his de-

Perhaps the shining example of some who were sleeping in such close proximity to James Monroe's law office, was something of an inspiration to his future great deeds.

scendants are still active in that church. He was twice married. His first wife was a Mildred Washington, it is said, and his second was Sarah Fontaine. Dr. Lawrence Berry Rose, who married Eliza Wellford, was a son of the latter union. One of the interesting old documents at the courthouse is a deed, made in 1814, transferring Lots 109-110, bounded by Charles, Fauquier, and Prince Edward Streets, to Alexander F. Rose. The lots (one-half acre each) at one time belonged to Fielding and Betty Lewis, and were "opposite to the property formerly occupied by Major Benjamin Day." When they were transferred to Alexander Rose, they were a part of the estate of the Hon. John Dawson, deceased, "the poor man's friend," and congressman from this district, who, according to the biographers of James Monroe, was connected with that eminent man. Although this year must have been about the climax of his (Monroe's) numberless pre-presidential engagements—for he now held either the office of Secretary of State or acting Secretary of War—he, with Robert Patton, the son-in-law of General Hugh Mercer, took time to administer the estate of his departed colleague, Hon. John Dawson. The latter was an important man in national affairs.

Tradition, which, in this case, has reasonable grounds for fact, says that James Monroe and John Dawson each lived in the old house with the enormous chimney, corner Fauquier and Prince Edward Streets, which recently has been demolished.

———

Rowe: Albert E., son of George and Lucy Rowe. Born December 17th, 1819. Died May 8th, 1848.

———

Rowe: In memory of George Rowe. Born Jan. 21st, 1793. Died Jan. 18th, 1866. Mark the perfect man, and behold the upright for the end of that man is Peace.

George Rowe was the ancestor of the well-known family of that name, who have contributed largely to the economic, social and civic interests of Fredericksburg. He was born in Stafford county. He must have well deserved the high tribute implied in his epitaph and also in the newspapers of that day. He was a Baptist minister by profession, and his main charge was Salem Church in Spotsylvania county. But his work with the colored Baptists in Fredericksburg will always be remembered. In 1854 the white congregation of that denomination left their church on Water Street to occupy their handsome new building on Princess Ann Street. They turned their old church over for the occupancy of their colored brethren, on which site they worship today. It was at this time and until the outbreak of the War Between the States that Rev. Mr. Rowe ministered to them. He died soon after the close of the war, and Rev. W. H. Williams officiated at his funeral services in the Baptist Church. Mr. Rowe built the house on upper Hanover Street, now occupied by his grandson, J. P. Rowe, and family, and was occupying it during the bombardment of Fredericksburg in 1862. He was a ponderous man, his weight being nearly three hundred pounds, while his wife, Lucy Leitch, was an unusually small woman. It was no uncommon sight, on the hills and dales of the surrounding country, to see the old family coach with its spring seat bending low to the ground on the one side, and on the other a bit elevated in the Spotsylvania ozone.

ROWE: In memory of James Montague, son of James and Lucy Rowe, who died June 26th, 1838. Aged 7 months & 19 days.

ROWE: In memory of John C., son of J. G. and M.
A. Rowe. Born Jan. 23rd, 1855. Died Feb.
9th, 1856. Of such is the kingdom of Heaven.

This baby was the grandson of Rev. George and Lucy Leitch Rowe and son of Rev. John G. and Margaret Ann Purcell Rowe. Rev. Mr. Rowe was a Methodist minister and was pastor of the churches in Westmoreland county, afterwards in Caroline county, where he served three separate terms. When he returned for the third time his opening sermon was from the first verse of the thirteenth chapter of Second Corinthians, "This is the third time I am coming to you."

———

ROWE: In memory of Lucy, beloved wife of George
Rowe. Born Feb. 22nd, 1798. Died March
27th, 1863. Her children arise up and call
her blessed, her husband also and he praiseth
her. Prov. 31 chap., 28 v.

Before her marriage Lucy Rowe was Lucy Leitch.

———

ROWE: Lucy A., Second daughter of Rev. John G.
& Margaret A. Rowe. Died Aug. 11th, 1851.
Aged 18 months . . . .

———

ROWE: In memory of Sarah E. Rowe, who departed this life the 26th of Feb., 1824. Aged 18 months and 15 days . . . .
 . . . . bud so sweet and fair.

This baby was doubtless named for Miss Sarah Leitch.

RUDD: To the memory of Hannah Rudd, who died May 16th, 1858. Aged 81 years.

Hannah Rudd was the "venerable and venerated mother of Captain John Rudd, U. S. Navy." Captain Rudd spent many years in Fredericksburg, being here between cruises. At one time he was with Captain David Porter, and in 1826 was ordered to the U. S. Ship *Brandywine*. In 1859 he commanded the Washington navy-yard. The Rudds were pew owners in St. George's Church. Their residence was the house on the corner of Princess Ann and Charlotte Streets.

RUDD: Departed this life on the 21st of April, 1843, Miss Mary Ann Rudd. Aged 45 years.

Thy tomb by Jesus' love is blest
Thy spirit to its Father God, hath winged its way.

Mary Rudd was probably the daughter of Mrs. Hannah Rudd.

SAVAGE: There is rest in Heaven. Sacred to the
memory of Susan A., Daughter of Jno. & Cath.
Metcalfe and wife of Rev. Tho's. S. Savage.
Born in Fredericksburg, and died April 16th,
1839, in the 28th year of her age, at Cape
Palmas, Western Africa, where her mortal remains now rest, waiting to be quickened into
life, when her Lord shall appear in his glory.

Rev. Philip Slaughter, the inspiring histo-
riographer of the Diocese of Virginia, of another day, counts it a privilege to have
known personally the one to whom this ceno-
taph is raised. In her early years she was
confirmed in St. George's Church, and Dr.
Slaughter says that her "walk was worthy
of her high vocation." She possessed those
qualities which commended her to that zealous pioneer in African missions, Dr. Thomas
S. Savage, to whom she was married in 1838,
in the house on Princess Street, now occupied by the Willis family. In December of
that year, she, with her husband, sailed for
Africa, where she died in April, 1839. Dr.
Slaughter thus characterizes her, "Who that
remembers that open face, that cheerful
voice, those artless manners, that kind and
gentle heart which so endeared her to the
social and domestic circles in which she
moved, but will drop a tear at the early
blighting of her bloom beneath the scorching

sun of Africa?" The suggestion that she did not live and die in vain is expressed by the same gifted man, in the following hope-laden prophesy, "If the blood of the martyrs be the seed of the church, from the graves of Launcelot Minor and Susan Savage there yet may spring a noiseless band of heavenly soldiery, who . . . will carry the war into Africa, and plant the ensigns of the gospel high on the pagan hills . . ."

(Rev. Launcelot Byrd Minor was the son of General John Minor, of Hazel Hill, and his wife, Lucy Landon Carter.)

Incidentally Rev. Thomas S. Savage, M. D., was the first white missionary to be sent by the Episcopal Church to foreign shores. He arrived, the first time, in Cape Palmas on Christmas day, 1836. He was a native of Connecticut and had practiced medicine.

Scott: Our Mother, Frances S. Scott.

Mrs. Frances Susannah Stone Payne Scott was the widow of John Scott, and the eldest daughter of Captain William Payne (Captain Pepper) of the Falmouth Blues, who won reputation during the Revolutionary War. The home of the Paynes was a mile or two north of Falmouth.

In her will, made in 1865, she mentions her daughters, Ann McC. Berry, Isabella R. Scott, Jannett H. Hamilton, and sons, John F., William S., Charles S., Hugh, and George B. She also mentions "the children of my daughter, the late Mrs. Susan Green." Robert T. Knox and James S. Knox were witnesses to her will. Mrs. Scott was born January 30, 1780, and died January 4, 1867.

Scott: Here lies the body of John Scott, who died Jan. 11th, 1848, in the 76th year of his age. Long one of the most respectable merchants in Fredericksburg. He was born in Greenock, Scotland, and emigrated to this country at a very early age. He possessed a large portion of that charity so beautifully described by St. Paul in the 13th chapter of his first epistle to Corinthians. Reader, look at this chapter for a knowledge of his character.

John Scott was the first of his family to come to this country. When a youth of sixteen he earnestly entreated his parents to allow him to try his fortune in the New World. From his request being granted, at that early age, one infers that the parents with prophetic vision, foresaw that the qualities combined in the boy were of such a nature as to preclude all doubt and uneasiness as to his conduct in a strange country.

He landed from the steamer in 1788, at Leedstown, Westmoreland county, at that time an important port on the Rappahannock River. He crossed to the Essex side, and found employment with the Brookes of Brooke's Bank, who had built up a large shipping trade from that point, mainly in tobacco. He was there for several years, until the death of Mr. Brooke. He then removed to Fredericksburg and entered into a business partnership with Robert Mackey, a fellow Scotchman and intimate friend. By mutual understanding there would be no speculating. John Scott considered it was not legitimate business. They were most successful. His next important step in life was to fall in love with Frances S. Stone Payne, to whom he was married October 14, 1799. He built for her the charming old home on Charles Street, *Scotia*, which, to the great regret of many, was wrecked more than three years ago. This old home was known through successive generations for its abounding hospitality. It was the center for all the connections and friends. After many years of happiness, prosperity and blessings, the half-score of promising children being the chief of which, a cloud sudden and lowering appeared on their horizon. Mr. Mackay could not resist a certain speculation. The speculation proved a failure, and the heretofore prosperous firm found itself without a penny to its credit, and with many liabilities. Many were the consultations between young Scott and his faithful and efficient wife as to schemes and plans to best face the future. And many were the discouraging days. (His cordial relations to Mr. Mackay under these difficult conditions prove the abounding charity with which he is accredited.)

But one evening when the cloud seemed darkest, and plans and schemes discussed until the hour was late, John Scott must have again become possessed of his magic wand. For apparently out of a starlit sky there appeared at the door of *Scotia* a very material form of fairy in the person of Cousin Anthony Christopher, a very wealthy and very dear relative ·from Scotland, who had just stepped from the Rappahannock steamer. He knew nothing of the business complications, but needless to say the whole of the night was spent in fruitful discussion, and "Cousin Christopher" was unofficial chairman of a ways and means committee. Next day the two men found themselves deep in consultation with officers of the old Bank of Virginia and other business houses, and before long Mr. Scott's business affairs were in an even more prosperous condition than before, "and they all lived happily" thereafter.

———

SHEPHERD: In memory of John M. Shepherd. Died in 1832. Aged 47 years. And of his wife, Judith Benson Shepherd. Died Feb. 16th, 1870, in her 80th year.

Many of the most substantial citizens of Fredericksburg are lineally descended from this worthy couple. Mr. Shepherd was a pew owner in St. George's Church in 1832. His father was Andrew Shepherd, of Orange county. A local writer calls Mr. Shepherd "the handsomest man ever seen," and adds that whenever he visited the home of one of the residents on Gunnery Green for the purpose of collecting taxes—on account of his attractive appearance and his expressed admiration of her flower garden, which was her pride and joy,—she cheerfully produced the money as though it were a great pleasure to pay taxes.

Mrs. Judith Benson Shepherd long survived her husband. She died at the residence of Captain R. H. Alexander, Mrs. Alexander being a near relative. Her sisters were Elizabeth or Betsy, who married James Timberlake, Catharine E. (Mrs. A. W. Wrenn), and Mary and Isabella Benson.

———

SLAUGHTER: Harriet Ficklen, infant daughter of Franklin and Lucretia Slaughter. Died July 27th, 1849.

The father of this child was a prominent citizen of Fredericksburg, a banker and president of the Old Dominion Steamboat Company.

———

SMITH: The remains of Mrs. Delia Smith, widow of George Smith, late of Dumfries, Virginia. Died April 8th, 1841, in the 59th year of her age. To our mother, Delia Smith. Born in Dumfries, Va., July 12, 1780. Died April 8, 1841. Aged 60 years, 8 months, and 27 days.

The parents of Mrs. Delia Forbes Smith were Dr. David Forbes, of Scotland—the first of the name to come to America—and his wife, Margaret Sterling, the only child of the last Laird, of Herbertshire. They were married in Edinburgh in 1774, and came to America and settled in Dumfries, Virginia. Dr. Forbes was a surgeon in the Revolution. Their daughter, Delia Forbes, was married to George Smith at Dumfries, November 28, 1799. Murray Forbes Smith, a son of this union, was married, May, 1840, in Mobile, Ala., to Miss Ann Desha, and their daughter, Alva, married William K. Vanderbilt, of New York City. She was afterwards Mrs. O. H.

P. Belmont. The former Duchess of Marlborough, Consuello Vanderbilt, was a great-granddaughter of Mrs. Smith.

Her will was probated in Fredericksburg in 1841. She conveys to her daughter, Sally Smith, and her heirs forever, all her property.

SMITH: Sacred to the memory of Penlope Smith, daughter of William and Mary Smith, who departed this life September 1st, 1802. Aged 1 year and 27 days.

SOMERVILLE: Sacred to the memory of James Somerville, a merchant of Fredericksburg, whose remains are here deposited. He was born in Glasgow, Scotland, the 25th February A. D. 1742, and departed this life at Port Royal on the 4th day of April, 1798.

James Somerville was the first of the name to come to Virginia. The paragraph in his will relating to the land where the Masonic burying-ground is located has been referred to. He was everywhere spoken of as being a wealthy merchant, Somerville & Mitchell being the firm name. James Somerville's executors were Walter Colquhoun of Falmouth, James Blair, Daniel Grinnan, Jr., and "my nephew, James Somerville, of Fredericksburg." To the latter he leaves lands in

Orange and Culpeper, which he recommends as "a healthy, agreeable, beautiful, and eligible Situation . . . which I would have freed and settled had I been married, or intended to marry." He also left to James Somerville, Jr., "one-half of the Copartnery business in which I have been engaged with my worthy and much respected Friend, General Edward Stevens, of Culpeper, carried on under the name of Stevens and Somerville, at Culpeper." Rev. Philip Slaughter, in his history of St. Mark's Parish, gives an account of General Stevens' services in the Revolution, and quotes the epitaph on his tomb at his old country seat near Culpeper (now the Masonic cemetery there). General Stevens died in 1820, devising by his will one acre of land near his own family burying-ground in Culpeper to be used as a cemetery for the members of Lodge No. 43, A. F. & A. M. (Fairfax Lodge, it was called).

There were no witnesses to the will of James Somerville, but James Miller, James Robb, and Jonathan Harris testified to his handwriting. He also mentions in his will "Lot No. 274, whereon I now live, with small warehouse . . . and stone wharf . . . purchased of Robert Johnston of Fredericksburg, but last of Portroyal . . ."

"My nephew, James Somerville, Jr.", married Mary Atwell, of Fauquier, and took possession of his inheritance on the Rapidan in 1810, giving it the euphonious and significant name *"Somervilla."*

Within the past few months a bronze plate, with name and dates, has been placed by relatives on the old warped stone to James Somerville's memory.

––––––

SPOONER: Henry A. A. Spooner. Died September, 1797. Aged 13 months.

The lapse of more than a century and a quarter had caused this little stone to sink in the ground until no letter was visible. But the pickaxe and trowel disclosed the above inscription, wonderfully preserved.

––––––

STANARD: Caroline M. Stanard. April 12th, 1863. Make her to be numbered with thy saints in glory everlasting.

Caroline M. Stanard was Caroline M. Chew, a sister of John Chew who is sleeping adjacent, and wife of Colonel John Stanard.

––––––

STANARD: Sacred to the memory of Hugh Claiborne Stanard, who departed this life the 15th of October, 1832, in the 11th year of his age. Jesus said, Suffer little children to come unto me, and forbid them not for of such is the kingdom of Heaven.

Hugh Claiborne was the son of Colonel John and Caroline M. Stanard.

STANARD: Sacred to the memory of Col. John Stanard. Aged 47 years. After he had served his country with reputation in stations military and civil, he enlisted under the banner of Emmanuel, gained the victory over sin and death, and departed with joy at the command of his Lord.

> Calm on the bosom of thy God,
> Fair spirit rest thee now,
> E'er while with ours thy footsteps trod
> His seal was on thy brow.
> Dust to its narrow house beneath
> Soul to its place on high
> They that have seen thy face in death
> No more may fear to die.

This monument has been erected as a testimony of conjugal affection by his bereaved widow.

Colonel John Stanard was born at Stanfield, Spotsylvania county, the residence of his father, Captain Larkin Stanard, and Elizabeth Perrott Chew, his wife. One reads

The shaft to the memory of Bazil Gordon stands to the right of the monument to Dr. James Carmichael.

Where the Stanards are sleeping.

between the lines of his epitaph the importance of his services to his country, and the obviously far-reaching effects of his example as a Christian gentleman. His official military life began as ensign, U. S. Infantry, 1807, captain in 1812, and lieutenant-colonel in 1814. He was honorably discharged June 15, 1815. A severe wound which lamed him for life was received in a duel with Dr. Bronaugh, an army surgeon. In 1824, at the time of the visit of Lafayette to this country, Colonel Stanard was one of the escort to meet him at Spotsylvania Courthouse and accompany him to Fredericksburg. It was he who fired the salute from the artillery stationed on the outskirts of the town, which announced to the citizens the approach of the great man. When President Jackson was here in May, 1833, on the occasion of the laying of the corner-stone of the first Mary Washington monument, the beautiful home of Colonel John Stanard was one whose doors were thrown wide open to the throng of distinguished guests. The beautiful lot on Princess Ann Street, on which is now the Shepherd residence, was, until 1814, the Stanard property, when Elizabeth Stanard, the widow of William, conveyed the lots (83-84) to Robert Mackey, who built the present handsome residence. Colonel Stanard was a member of the Presbyterian Church here in 1833.

The *Richmond Whig* of September 27, 1833, quotes the following from a Fredericksburg paper: "It is with sincere regret we announce the death of Colonel John Stanard, of this town, formerly of the army of the United States, and later marshal of the Chancery Court of the Fredericksburg district."

STONE: In memory of Mildred Stone . . . . (defaced and illegible).

This is probably Milly Richards Stone,* the daughter of John Richards, of Richards' Hill, Stafford county, who married William Scandrett Stone, a highly esteemed merchant of Fredericksburg, mayor of the town in 1801, an active member of Lodge No. 4, a

---

* Circumstantial, if not positive evidence from members of the family led me to believe that this stone marked the last resting place of the wife of William S. Stone. But this supposition is now shattered by the discovery that some years ago William S. and Milly Stone were removed from the Masonic burying-ground, and now sleep in the Fredericksburg City Cemetery. Two horizontal stones mark their memory. On one is a glowing tribute, and I am sure it is well deserved, to William Stone. But on the companion one, touching his, there is only this uncommunicative phrase, "To My Mother".

As long as she once occupied a spot here where the subject of these sketches sleep, it will not be out of place to include a sketch of Milly Stone and her interesting and prolific family.

It cannot be ascertained who is this Mildred Stone, but I am of the opinion that she is one of this lineage.

vestryman in the Episcopal Church, a lay delegate to the Episcopal Convention in 1812, and again in 1821. They had a large family of ten children, and lived for a few years at White Plains, that still pretty old place, on the Richmond-Washington highway, just outside of Fredericksburg and adjoining Bunker Hill.

The children who survived their youth were William, who married a Miss Benson and removed to Kentucky; Evelina, married Charles Henry Smith, of Norfolk; Margaret Emmilly, married Dr. William Browne, of Windsor, Stafford county (a daughter of this couple, Milly Stone Browne, married Lieutenant-Governor John L. Marye, Jr.); Louisa Richards, married her cousin, J. R. Triplett, of Richmond; Susan Catharine, married Thomas B. Barton, Esq. (Judge William S. Barton was a son of this union); Milly, married William Fairfax Gray and went to Houston, Tex. (Mrs. Temple Doswell, Evelina, was a daughter of this couple), and Mary, married Thomas Hutchinson Botts, from whom descended Albert B., Charles Minor, Benjamin Botts, and others.

The "Stone girls" were noted far and wide for their beauty, and if one could uncover several score of vanished years he would doubtless see that big, rambling old frame dwelling on Princess Ann Street, the center of culture and accomplishment, and also of lavish hospitality, as it was of later years when the Barton family had it in possession. This charming and typical old Southern home was called by some wit *"The Quarry,"* and it retained its name for years. It was razed about fifteen years ago, and the Princess Ann Hotel now has possession of the site.

———

STORKE: To the memory of William Storke, who died Aug. 27th, 1822. Aged 69 years. This stone is placed by his bereaved widow. But we sorrow not as those who have no hope, For if we believe that Jesus died and rose again, even so them also which sleep in Jesus will God bring with him.

William Storke's will provides that his wife, Anna Rosetta Byron Storke, shall have that "parcel of land where I now reside known as Bunker's Hill." He also leaves her plentifully supplied with slaves, calling them all by name. Upon the death of Mrs. Storke, Bunker Hill passed into the hands of a son, William Storke. Frances Hooe Johnston was a daughter, and other sons were Henry D. and Bailey Washington. They occupied pew No. 33 in St. George's Church—the building erected in 1814. Bunker Hill still occupies its pretty location just midway between Fredericksburg and Falmouth.

The Storkes were of the family of Bailey Washington, and his gallant son, Lieutenant-Colonel William Augustine Washington, of Stafford county.

TAYLOR: Our little babe, Evalyn Wallace, daughter of Joshua T. and Maria L. Taylor. Aged 1 month and 15 days.

TAYLOR: M. Louisa, wife of J. T. Taylor, daughter of A. & C. Kale. Died in Washington, D. C., Dec. 8th, 1872, in her 54th year.

Gone but not forgotten.

The semi-weekly *Herald* of December 19, 1872, has this notice: "Died, in Washington, D. C., December 8, 1872, Marie Louise, wife of Joshua T. Taylor, and oldest daughter of the late Anthony T. Kale, of Fredericksburg, Virginia. Her remains were brought to this place, and the funeral services took place at St. George's Episcopal Church . . ."

URQUHART: In memory of William Lovell Urquhart,
born Feb. 22nd, 1791. Died Nov., 1793.

This may have been the little son of
Charles Urquhart, who was a prominent
member of St. George's vestry, and removed
from the parish in 1793, possibly to Port
Royal. Charles Urquhart was the grantor
of many pieces of property here between the
years 1788 and 1825.

WALKER: In memory of Alexander Walker, born
July 1st, 1771, died September 28th, 1830.
Aged 59 years, 2 months and 29 days.

In an old edition of the *Virginia Herald* is
an advertisement of Windsor chairs for sale
by Alexander Walker, cabinetmaker. The
"shop," the description of which implying big
business, mentioned in his will, made August
18, 1830, leads one to believe that the Alexander Walker sleeping here was the cabinetmaker. The belief is somewhat strength-
ened by the fact that two chairs were purchased from a Miss Walker, thirty or forty
years ago, by Lodge No. 4, which had once
been in possession of Mrs. Mary Ball Washington, the mother of the General, and which
are still valued relics of the Masonic Lodge.

Alexander Walker mentions among many

other items in his will, his plantation in Stafford, his lots in Fredericksburg, "purchased of Mary and John Coakley." He gives "the house and lot I now occupy, including the shop thereon, in which I now carry on my business, to my beloved wife Susan," also fifteen servants, and all the other servants (calling them all by name) "that work in the shop." He leaves his wife everything necessary to carrying on the business, tools, material, stock in trade, etc. He wants his son, Richard, to continue the business for his mother, and he desires that the "infant part of my family be particularly well taken care of." His wife Susan, his son Richard, and John Metcalfe are his executors.

William W. Spindler, Robert C. Bruce, William Murphy, witnesses.

WALKER: In memory of Catherine Walker, daughter of Alexander and Susan Walker. Born Sept. 7th, 1820, Died Oct. 8th, 1821. Aged 1 year and 30 days.

WALKER: In memory of Edgar, infant son of Harris and Mar⁴ Walker, who departed this life June, 1830. Aged 11 months and 7 days.

WALKER: Our mother, Susan Walker. Born 18th
     November, 1782. Died 16th February, 1865.
     Aged 83 years.

Mrs. Walker lived many years after her
husband, Alexander Walker.

———

WALKER: In memory of William Alexander Walker,
     who departed this life June 26th, 1805. Aged
     22 months.

also

Sarah Ann Walker, who departed this life July
9th, 1806. Aged 12 months.

———

WALKER: Sacred to the memory of William Cald-
     well, the son of Harris and Margaret Walker,
     who departed this life May 30th. Aged 4
     years and 9 months.

———

WALLACE:

It seems almost unbelievable that a man
who had been given the important role of
acting Brigadier-General for a short space of
time, and of Lieutenant-Colonel during the
greater part of the American Revolution,
should be sleeping today with not a letter
of his illustrious name to mark his last
resting place. But such is the case with Lieu-

Entrance to the old Rising Sun Tavern, once owned by Lieut. Colonel Gustavus B. Wallace. The red silk scarf worn by him during the Revolution is on the porch railing.

tenant-Colonel Gustavus Brown Wallace. He was born at Ellerslie, King George county, Va. (now Stafford county), November 9, 1751. He was one of six brothers, all commissioned officers in the American Revolution. Colonel Wallace was taken prisoner at the fall of Charleston, S. C., and carried aboard a British man-of-war. There he met Sir Henry Clinton, who effected an interview for him with Lord Cornwallis as to a parole which Colonel Wallace greatly desired. His wish was granted and Lord Cornwallis signed the papers himself. In his will, made December 19, 1794, he says: "I give my soul to Him who gave it to me, my body I bequeath to my brethren of the Fredericksburg Lodge who I hope will inter me as a Mason, in the Burying-Ground." He wants Patrick McCarty educated, and desires "my servant woman Linnsy to be emancipated." He gives "the residue of my estate" to a relative, Elizabeth Spooner. G. W. B. Spooner, his brother Thomas Wallace, David Henderson, William Drummond, Hazlewood Farish, Samuel Smith and others are mentioned as either executors or witnesses. Colonel Wallace never married. In 1802 he went abroad to look after his interest in some property, and after a short stay over there, he contracted typhoid fever on shipboard coming home. He went, as soon after landing as possible, to the home of his cousin, Mrs. Travers Daniel, of Crow's Nest, King George county, who brought him in her carriage to the old tavern on Main Street, this city, now the Rising Sun Tavern, of which he was owner. He died a few days after and was buried as he had requested, in this cemetery, with

> His spirit to God,
> His memory in our hearts,
> His body to the earth.

> His spirit to God,
> His memory in our hearts,
> His body to the earth.

> His spirit to God,
> His memory in our hearts,
> His body to the earth.

WELLFORD: This stone is placed at the head of Edward Robert Wellford, son of William and Susan. Born June 28th, 1812, and died 20th Sept., 1814. Aged 2 years, 2 months and 23 days.

WELLFORD. Sacred may this marble long remain the just tribute of a wife's affection for the memory of a deeply regretted husband. William Wellford willingly obeyed Death's awful summons on the 3rd of June, 1817, in the 33rd year of his age. Much did he suffer in mind and body during a long illness and when the clay tabernacle was shaken to its foundation and about to fall into the grave, it pleased Almighty God to unfold to him the riches of his grace and the all-sufficiency of the atonement of His Son. Encouraged by this he cast himself on the mercy of a forgiving God and departed in the full assurance of happiness in a better world.

While weeping friends bend o'er the silent tomb
Recount his virtues, and his loss deplore,
Faith's piercing eye darts through the dreary
gloom
And calls him blest where tears shall flow no
more.

Near him is interred all that was mortal of Francis John, second son of William and Susan Wellford. At an early age he was taken from the evil to come.

Mr. William Wellford was a merchant of Fredericksburg and the second son of Dr. Robert Wellford and his wife, Catharine Yates, the widow Thornton.

WHITE: In memory of Catherine Hannah, Daughter of Henry and Elizabeth White. Ob. 3rd of July, 1817. Æ. 15 months and 27 days.

This must be an infant daughter of "Mr. Harry White" who married "Miss Betsy Peacock." The grandfather of this baby was Captain Peacock, a soldier of the Revolution.

————

WHITE: In memory of Henry White, who departed this life April 28th, 1827, in the 68th year of his age.

Henry White made his will March 25, 1826. He mentions his wife and younger children, Susan and Sarah Ann. He appoints his wife and son, William, and his friend, George Rothrock, executors to his will.

Garrit Minor, James Dixon, witnesses.

————

WHITE: Henry White. O. B., July, 1806. Æ, 6 months.

————

WHITE: Sarah White, wife of Henry White. Departed this life Jan. 29th, 1802, in the 29th year of her age.

————

WILSON: In memory of Ellen Gordon Wilson, daughter of Douglas H. Gordon and Mary Ellen Clarke. Born Nov. 30, 1848. Died March 3, 1894.

Mrs. Wilson was a granddaughter of Bazil and Anna Campbell Gordon, of Falmouth.

WOODVILLE: Underneath is the body of John Woodville, a true believer in the Holy Scriptures, an earnest minister of the Protestant Episcopal Church, a diligent and faithful teacher of youth, a meek, contented, cheerful sojourner on earth, a pious probationer, and an humble candidate of heaven. In Anglia natus die Martii undecimo MDCCLXIII. Obiit Virginia undecimo die Januarii MDCCCXXXIV.

Rev. John Woodville was born in White Haven, Cumberland county, England, in 1763, came to America in 1787, and became a tutor in the family of Rev. James Stevenson. He was ordained to the priesthood in Philadelphia, 1788, and soon thereafter became master of the Academy in Fredericksburg. He was elected rector of St. George's Church in 1792. Resigning this charge in 1794, he became rector of St. Mark's Parish, Culpeper.

Mr. Woodville married Sarah, daughter of Rev. James Stevenson, who was the niece of

General Lewis Littlepage. So great was his love and admiration for the latter great historical figure that he expressed his desire to be brought back to Fredericksburg at his death, and laid to rest near him. The following paragraph from Bishop Meade shows his esteem for Mr. Woodville: "On the 4th of September, 1834,* I preached to a large congregation at the Little Fork in Culpeper ... under the care of Rev. Mr. Woodville ... here I saw him for the last time ... I often met him in my travels during the last 22 years ... He has left an affectionate family to mourn the loss of a kind husband and father and many friends to cherish with sincere respect the memory of a conscientious Christian."

---

* There is a discrepancy in this date as Mr. Woodville died in January, 1834.

YATES: In memory of Charles Yates. He was a native of White Haven and departed this life the 11th of January, 1809, in the 81st year of his age, after a long and painful illness which he endured with the fortitude and resignation of a Christian. Few have lived more respectably, or better deserved respect. Sincere in his friendships, Warm in his attachments, an indulgent master, Hospitable, charitable and benevolent, just and of the strictest probity, Liberal without ostentation, Generous but not profuse, Sympathetic where sympathy's aid could best afford relief, To pity the distrest inclin'd, as well as just to all mankind.

The name, Charles Yates, is a familiar one on the old rolls of Fredericksburg's past records. He was a zealous member of Fredericksburg Lodge of Masons, serving as secretary, and as junior warden for a long period of time. He is listed on the roster of members from Allen Town in Spotsylvania. It is recorded on September 6, 1756, at one of the many meetings of the Lodge at Charles Julian's in the county: "This night Bro. Yates paid up, being the entrance money for his being made a member of this Lodge." For many years thereafter his name is never missing among the list of members present. Among his Masonic contemporaries, who were also generally regular at the meetings, were Fielding Lewis, James Mercer, Hugh Mercer, Charles Dick, John Thornton, Lewis Willis, George Weedon, and others of note.

The old will of Charles Yates is an interesting document, proved in 1809. He probably never married, and evidently had a great deal of property both in this country and in England. He leaves "lands and real estate" in Virginia to his nephew, John Yates, the son of his brother, John Orseur Yates. Among the many other legacies to this nephew are, "my gold ring which was the wedding ring of my grandmother Yates . . . my gold ring with my coat of arms engraved . . ." He leaves $2,000 to the Fredericksburg Charity School, "for educating poor boys," and $1,000 to his god-daughter, Christian Yates Day. The nieces and nephews of Daniel Payne and the children of William Payne (Colonel Payne of the Falmouth Blues) are remembered generously. He leaves $1,000 to each of the children of John Scott, because of their "blood connection with the same William Payne." To Aminadab Booker, "my now hired servant," and to various other colored folk, he leaves money. To his nephew, Rev. Richard Mathews, of Wigton, county of Cumberland, England, and nieces of the same name, he gives a goodly heritage. He desires Major Benjamin Day to be his executor in Virginia, and bequeaths to him, amongst other things, his "printed books . . .," his sleeve buttons with his "cypher engraved on them."

After many pages of bequests, he says: "Twentiethly . . . I have great confidence in the integrity of Benjamin Day, my executor in Virginia . . .," and, "Lastly, I appoint my aforesaid nephew, the Rev. Richard Mathews, of Wigton my sole executor in England. . . ." Anno Domini . . . 1806. Witnesses, Timothy Green, John Mundell, John Brown, and Donald Campbell.

It is interesting to glance through the old records and find among the grantors and grantees, the names of those capable business men, who rest in the holy ground of Fredericksburg Lodge, said to be the oldest Masonic cemetery in America. In reading over the old wills, how the living soul is stirred with a feeling of veneration for those saints who desire so fervently the happiness and welfare of their loved ones! Freedom or adequate provision for their slaves is, too, a point often stressed. And almost invariably, if there are young children, their education is carefully considered and definitely provided for.

With Charles Yates ends the list of those who have their names chiselled in the marble of this old burying-ground, and several have been given prominence where no stone records their name. Possibly there sleep here in the hospitable bosom of old Mother Earth some unidentified souls, whose names are written in capital letters in the annals of the State. Circumstances or conditions, and sometimes thoughtlessness, and unwarranted carelessness or indifference are reasons for not honoring their memory. It does seem, in some cases, as though no condition could justify the omission of the name and the date at least.

Other persons besides those recorded, to be found in church or courthouse records, who are buried herein are John Minor, son of General John Minor, whose sturdy and still beautiful old home on lower Main Street is still pointed out as the one in which his relatives, the family of Commodore Matthew Fontaine Maury resided during the War Between the States; Mrs. Elizabeth Carmichael, the widow of Dr. James Carmichael; Miss Ann Hackley; Miss Isabella Scott, of Scotia; Miss Lucy H. Metcalfe, daughter of John Metcalfe, Esq.; Mrs. Eliza Alexander Roy, widow of John Roy; Major W. T. Dix, of the Confederate States Army, and others. There are also handsome stones with the apparently meaningless inscriptions, "Ida," "Maggie," "Willie", encircled by a wreath of blossoms artistically chiselled into the stone.

Rev. Philip Slaughter says: "We are glad that there is a spot where all men of all creeds can come, leaving their Shibboleths behind them, and within whose gates, no voice of discord is heard to mar the music of the birds, and of the tuneful winds playing their requiems upon the evergreen harps of holly and of yew."